DRAGOM i POŠTOVANOM PRIJATELJU – PAŠENOGU DANIEL-u CALABRESE, ZA USPOMENU i PODSJEĆANJE NA NEPROLAZNE PRIRODNE LJEPOTE (SVJETSKE RARITETE) i KULTURNO-ISTORISKU BAŠTINU RODNOG ZAVIČAJA SVOJE SUPRUGE ANDELKE, ZA UPOZNAVANJE NJENIH KORIJENA, SA ISKRENOM ŽELJOM DA LIČNO POSJETI CRNU GORU, dožio je i STVARNO NA LICE MJESTA, DA UPOZNA ŽENINU ROĐBINU i BUDE NAŠ GOST.

SRdačno, i s' dubokim uvažavanjem,
DRAGUTIN-DRAGO BOGIĆEVIĆ. –
PODGORICA, jula 1998.

MONTENEGRO

Photographs on the preceding pages:
1. The Gulf of Kotor (Boka Kotorska)
2. Pržno, a tourist resort on the Budva riviera
3. Sveti (St.) Stefan, a hotel-village
4. Crno Jezero (Lake Crno - Black) in Durmitor National Park

5. The Sušica canyon, Mt. Durmitor
6. Skadarsko Jezero (Lake Skadar), the largest in the Balkans, a national park
7. "Rocky desert": Mali Žurim peak, Mt. Lukavica
8. Lake Sušičko depression on Mt. Durmitor, dry when water drains

MONTE

ecological

MIODRAG VARTABEDIJAN, Design

STUDIO STRUGAR

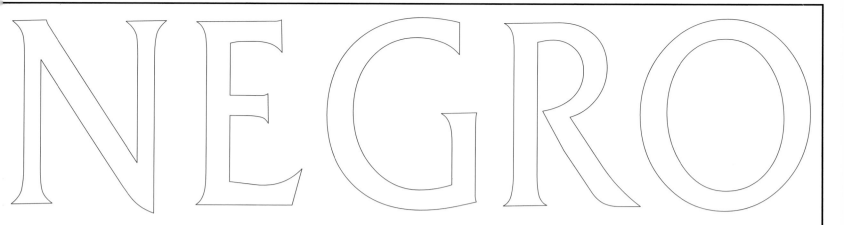

NEGRO

state

MOMIR BULATOVIĆ, Author   BRANISLAV STRUGAR, Photography

The Contributors:

MOMIR BULATOVIĆ
MILO ĐUKANOVIĆ,
SVETOZAR MAROVIĆ
MOMČILO STOJANOVIĆ
VLADISLAV A ŠANIN

Collaborators:

BOJKA ĐUKANOVIĆ, Ph D
RATKO ĐUROVIĆ, Ph D
VESNA KILIBARDA, Ph D
DUŠAN MARTINOVIĆ, Ph D
RADOSAV RASPOPOVIĆ, Ph D
KRUNOSLAV SPASIĆ, Ph D
LENKA ČELEBIĆ, M A

Project Secretary
MOMČILO STOJANOVIĆ

Editor–in–chief
JANKO BRAJKOVIĆ

Editor
VLATKA RUBINJONI STRUGAR

Photographic Editor
BRANISLAV STRUGAR

Technical Editor
SLAVKO MANDIĆ

CONTENTS

*M*ontenegro - Ecological State, for many people represents an enigma. I trust and hope that after meeting this book there will be more of those who understand at least a part of this great and noble idea which has been adopted on the soil of Montenegro. Since Montenegro, a small state in the south of the Balkans, is the first country in the world to announce its intention to be and to develop itself as an Ecological State.

In its whole essence Montenegro is a collection of sharp contrasts. Geographically small but enormous in relation to history, its cherished statehood and spiritual accomplishments which are a constituent part of the world's civilized inheritance. Montenegro is a state insufficiently known in the world, yet lauded and praised by many world known artists, travel writers, and statesmen. Exceptionally richly gifted with natural beauty, Montenegro has been heavily punished by the material poverty in which its inhabitants have lived.

At the end of the twentieth century Montenegro for the first time in its history has set out on the path of democratic development. The first freely elected parliament almost unanimously adopted the Declaration on the Ecological State, which as an idea, a project and a future way of life, represents the philosophy of development in this region. All differences between us as people with our own views, recorded then, are minor compared with the need to live in harmony with nature, and to protect ourselves and the world, (which doesn't belong to us since we have only borrowed it from our ancestors and owe it to our descendants) from pollution and destruction.

I sincerely believe that this is the right answer to the problem imposed on the whole world by modern development and the price it demands. For me personally it's an exceptionally happy circumstance and honour that I have had the opportunity to affirm and promote this idea and project in many and various ways, an idea which is worthy of investing one's whole time and effort, despite the fact that the project is so large and complex that one man, even one generation, can't give it its complete meaning and importance.

MOMIR BULATOVIĆ
President of the
Republic of Montenegro

The history of Montenegro is a history of wars and struggle for freedom. Montenegrins are famous as exceptional warriors who not only strongly desired, but also knew how to fight to achieve freedom and justice. The local heroes and warriors transformed their natural human fears into bravery. The giants of the mind have shown how quite simple, and ultimately comprehensible to all, solutions can stand behind large dilemmas and problems. Artists have given the human race works which transform the monotonous day to day into the permanent glory of creative beauty.

By its decision to direct its future development towards the Ecological State, Montenegro has turned its great deficiency into an unattainable advantage. The deficiency is material undevelopment and the lack of modern technology. The advantage is, exactly because of this, nature untouched and unharmed to a level difficult to grasp for many from modern and rich societies. The divine sanctity and primordial purity of this region won't be threatened by development and human activities. Seeing that what Montenegro has represents a rare jewel, the motives behind removing existing ecological black spots are powerful and well thought out. Montenegro is a member of many international societies and associations of experts in which it wants to learn and exchange experiences with others who work on ecological projects and programmes. Ecology is a future which has already started long ago. Not only does the past belong to Montenegro but also a significant role in the global future.

This book is intended to show the most important parts of the beauty which has been given to Montenegro, the unrepeatable natural riches, the generousity and good intentions of the people who live here. Thus this book is also a friendly invitation, offered to the hands of all who know, or are just getting to know this small-large country. It is also an expression of the traditional hospitality afforded to all those of good intention who have come to visit Montenegro. This book is a warm welcome sent into the world which has, respected reader, arrived at its ultimate destination - in your hands and thoughts.

*T*here is an old wise saying that the man (and nation) who has an aim in which he believes deeply has strength at his disposal of which he has no inkling. Thus at the time of the tragic breakup of the former Yugoslavia, the civil war in Bosnia and Croatia, and under international sanctions, the vision of Montenegro as an ecological state was an essential civilized step forward and a pillar of our strong orientation to peace, in the spirit of tolerance, rationality and the humanity of Montenegro towards its people and surroundings.

In proclaiming Montenegro an Ecological State in September 1991 the Montenegrin parliament set out for the future its relationship with nature, and also the position of Montenegro in international relations. In the economic sense this relationship may be expressed through the harmonising of development with nature or constant development, with that level of ecological sovereignty which enables an open economic climate, capable of being included in the process of European integration and capable of accepting high standards of development and ethics in business. In the sociological sense this is equally both a right and the possibility of choice for all, alongside an equal distribution of the common wealth. In the political sense this relationship is principally defined by peace and coexistence, a high level of political, religous and other tolerance, and a constant improvement of democratic institutions and processes.

The pioneer task of realizing the project Montenegro Ecological State is defined by the fundamental strategic elements of an Ecological State. These are: definition, which explains what is the aim of setting up an ecological state and the level of ecological sovereignty; organisation, which assumes regulations, a political and social-economic system, the economy, superstructure and institutions; physiognomy, which implies the appearance of nature and objects; and function, which assumes the separation of all functions of the Ecological State which are inter-linked, amongst which can be specially recognised economic activity in the area of the protection of the natural environment and the type of economic production.

MILO ĐUKANOVIĆ
Prime Minister of the
Republic of Montenegro

With the aim of popularizing the idea and attracting foreign investment the government of Montenegro is planning a strategy of marketing, international contacts, and cooperation with the appropriate agencies of the UN and other foreign governmental and non-governmental organisations, which are particularly significant in the consolidation and realisation of a series of sub-projects such as: legal regulations, a catalogue of natural treasures, a catalogue of polluters of the environment, natural potential, ecological sub-projects, and expert advice. Finally, Project Ecological State envisages raising of the general level of education and training amongst the population and the introduction of ecological education into schools and universities.

It is clear that we are embarking on a large, complex and long-term process with a series of different activities which will need to be synchronised and carried out with a high level of cooperation between the state, the private sector and ecological centres. The support and understanding of the international community, institutions and individuals who are prepared to join us and to take part in building a higher quality, richer and more worthy society is crucial in achieving this above all else human-centred project.

I hope that this book will increase the number of those showing interest in coming to Montenegro, getting to know it and strengthening its intentions in the area of ecology. I believe that many will feel the need to be our guests, or to become our fellow citizens, and I am certain that, if they do this, they will find in Montenegro expert colleagues, interested partners and people ready for business and cooperation.

M. Đukanović

10

9.
The Gulf of Kotor
10.
Sveti Nikola Island off Pržno
11.
Golden sea of the Budva riviera

11

At the moment of birth of our planet, the most
beautiful meeting of land and sea was on the
Montenegrin coast...
When the pearls of nature were sown, on this soil
an overflowing handful was gathered.
Lord Byron (1788 - 1824), English poet

D E C L A R A T I O N
ON THE ECOLOGICAL STATE OF MONTENEGRO

We, members of the Parliament of the Republic of Montenegro, are aware that, in view of the threat to nature, protection of the identity of the land in which we live and work has become our most immediate and pressing task.

Bearing in mind our debt to nature, a source of health and our inspiration for freedom and culture, we are devoting ourselves to its protection for the sake of our survival and the future of our posterity.

We recognize that all our differences are less important than the changes in the environment we live in. Regardless of our national, religious, political and other sentiments and convictions we are fully aware that dignity and blessedness of a human being are intrinsically connected with blessedness and purity of nature.

Man and creation in him and around him are one in their depths, their meaning and denotation.

Thus the abuse of man has always entailed the abuse of nature. And being committed to the struggle for the dignity of man, we are also called upon to struggle for the dignity of nature.

By adopting this Declaration, Montenegro defines its attitude towards nature as a state policy and calls upon all the people to show wisdom and prevent an impending ecological catastrophe.

Žabljak, 20 September 1991

THE PARLIAMENT
OF THE REPUBLIC OF MONTENEGRO

THE ECOLOGICAL STATE
A DREAM WHICH IS BECOMING A REALITY

*The road which leads to the Ecological
State is long and uncertain. This
generation won't be able to reach
its end. But we owe it to future
generations to set out on it.*

What is an Ecological State and what right has Montenegro to be the first (and until now only) country in the world to proclaim its intention to become one? Maybe the answer lies hidden in Montenegro's unique history and its own unique example of the development of civilisation over the centuries.

In Montenegrin tradition there exists a system of values which unerringly define the aims one should live for and for which it is worth fighting. The greatest aim of this people is freedom. Freedom from the powerful who would want to control its destiny, but also a freedom in which every one can offer their best for the promotion and development of their family, their people and their state. Great aims have always demanded proportional efforts and much time. But Montenegrins have, which history without any doubt proves, for generations ("from father to son") gone step by step towards their ideal.

This is why it was possible for the idea of the Ecological State to become so widely accepted. The creation of a state devoted to the inseparable unity of man and nature is an aim which exceeds the current knowledge of not only the citizens of Montenegro, but also that of all civilisation. Bearing in mind its own right and responsibility to add to the efforts to save the planet, but recognising its own aims and responsibilities, the parliament of Montenegro passed the Declaration of Montenegro as an Ecological State. The idea itself has been noted by many well respected people, institutions and international forums. At the World Ecological Summit in Rio de Janeiro (1992) the efforts of Montenegro drew special attention. Many at that time, for the first time seeing the ambition in the complete idea, curbed their initial doubts and showed an interest in getting to know Montenegro and enriching her reserves of ideas, ecological proposals and concrete actions.

The declaration of the Montenegrin parliament has been classified as an official document of the United Nations and has entered the treasury of universally accepted ideas for the salvation of the planet to which we belong.

The constitution of Montenegro states that it is a democratic, social and ecological state. Thus is expressed the belief that nature is the source of health, spirituality and culture for the human race, and the state protects the sanctity and purity of nature.

The constitution guarantees everyone the right to a healthy living environment, and the right to complete and quick access to information about its status. Everyone has the responsibility to protect and improve the environment. The freedom of companies is limited in the area of environmental protection, and each company, obviously committed to growth and economic success, is under the strong stimulus of state regulatory organisations.

Montenegro therefore by its constitution, laws, everyday practice and special educational system is seeking to protect and safeguard its most valuable resource. It is protecting the crystal clear air of its mountains, the clarity of its lakes and rivers, the blueness of it sea, the centuries-present flora and fauna, the laughter and health of its children.

Man and nature in him and around him, announced the Montenegrin parliament, are a complete whole in their significance and meaning. Thus a calling to fight for man's freedom and dignity is also a calling to fight for the dignity of nature. Ecology is, understood in this way, a modern way of expressing the centuries-old aspirations and spiritual longing of people from the rocks, mountains and sea to survive honourably, while protecting what is most valuable in themselves, but also around themselves. The tradition, heroism, ethics and chivalry of

Montenegrins didn't know about ecology, but they carried an identical message in its full expression of this modern imperative.

Montenegro - Ecological State is a vision but also a hope and a concrete programme. This vision contributes to the understanding and acceptance of real natural and human values existing in this region and which are worth protecting and developing.

However this big and magnificent idea from the tiny and insufficiently well known Montenegro will sound like a drop in the ocean to many. For of what significance is the purity of our rivers and the cleanliness of the air we breathe in comparison with the tons of chemicals and smog which the world industrial machine throws out daily into the atmosphere? And of course there are many other barriers which exist and which will arise before our dream becomes a reality.

Notwithstanding this, there are more reasons for the creation of the Ecological State. Regardless of the trials met by individual generations, it is always the right (seeing that it is the only) time to live and to think about life. If it were not so, life would lose its fundamental meaning. Alongside this, although man is not entirely master of his destiny, it is still his responsibility to do all he can to be a worthy descendant of his ancestors and ancestor of his descendants.

And this is why we decided to create the Ecological State - Montenegro. We are conscious of the philosophical, sociological, legal, economic and other aspects of this phenomenon. Behind each of our practical decisions stands a well thought out analysis, a weighing of the positive and negative ecological effects, as well as of long-term and ecological profitability as opposed to solutions which provide quick economic benefits. We are opening the door to all inventiveness, brave creativity and free imagination. All who wish to live, work and to earn in a healthy and protected environment are welcome in Montenegro, everyone who is conscious of the need of a post-industrial society and who, while wanting to earn a living, respect our cultural, spiritual and religous traditions. Montenegro is a home for all that is "green" in this world, all ideologies, faiths, cultures and philosophies... Since ecology best proves that the ethics of modern man must be the ethics of goodness and tolerance. My good can only be a part of the general good, and my freedom isn't freedom as far as it is at the expense of others.

The path we have to go along to truly create the Ecological State is incredibly complex, long and untrodden. This generation can't complete the journey. But for the sake of future generations we must set out along it.

12. Lake Plav

*There are several accounts
as to how the name of Montenegro came into
existence. According to one legend Montenegro
owes its present name to seafarers,
who spotted the region so close to
the sea yet completly cut off from it by
forbidding mountains rising straight
from the shore. Enveloped by clouds
and constantly beaten
by the elements these mountains appeared
to mariners as huge dark elevations.
Hence the "black mountain".*

A LAND OF 6 CONTINENTS

ontenegro is in many ways a unique corner of the earth. This is equally true of its geography and its people. Though it covers only 13,800 sq km and has a population of slightly over 600,000. Montenegro has made a significant contribution to the world's cultural heritage.

Support for this seemingly bold claim can be found in any of Montenegro's regions and in any period of its existence.

A Balkan state, Montenegro has survived centuries of turbulent history. Situated at the crossroads of ancient overland and sea routes, it has brought together a multitude of cultural, religious and ethnic influences. Its cultural and historical heritage is a nexus of pagan, Christian and Muslim beliefs and of Illyrian, Roman, Byzantine, Turkish and Slavic achievements.

What is nowadays called Montenegro (literally, "black mountain") - or Crna Gora in Serbian - has gone by many different names in the course of its long and stormy history. Its current name superseded the medieval appellation of Zeta. There are several accounts as to how this happened.

According to one legend, Montenegro owes its present name to seafarers, who spotted a region so close to the sea yet completely cut off from it by forbidding mountains rising straight from the shore. Enveloped by clouds and constantly beaten by the elements, these mountains appeared to mariners as huge dark elevations. Hence the "black mountain".

According to another legend, Montenegro's present name originated with its enemies, as an allusion to the grim fate befalling their armies in the mountains of this country.

But the name Montenegro most likely derives from the name of the Crnojevic family, Zeta's last medieval rulers. A Turkish onslaught forced them to move their seat from the fertile plain into the impenetrable hills enclosing present-day Cetinje. The fall of the Crnojevic dynasty and the state of Zeta left the people with the name "Crnojevica gora" ("the mountain of the Crnojevic's"), later shortened to "Crna Gora".

Montenegro is part of the central Mediterranean region and southern Europe. Together with the Republic of Serbia it constitutes the Federal Republic of Yugoslavia. It borders Albania in the southeast. The Adriatic Sea separates it from Italy in the south, while its western neighbours are the former Yugoslav republics of Croatia and Bosnia-Herzegovina.

Approximately 500 km separates Montenegro from Rome, about 1,500 from Paris and Berlin, close to 2,000 km from Moscow and nearly 7,500 km from New York.

GEOGRAPHIC AREAS AND CONTRASTS

Still, many famous people from far-away countries, undaunted by great distances, have visited Montenegro and enjoyed its singular beauty. Also, many Montenegrins have travelled to the world's largest cities, bringing part of their homeland with them in their hearts.

Those were the beginnings of Montenegro's fame. Its exquisite qualities and almost unbelievable contrasts have earned it the title of a LAND OF SIX CONTINENTS. It is not known when the phrase was first used, but there is no doubt that whoever coined it was absolutely right; for, it is difficult to find another country where so many different things co-exist in so small area.

The two farthermost points in Montenegro are only 190 km apart in a straight line, but between them the North Pole and the Equator seem to meet. Exotic tropical trees grow not far from Alpine plants. Snow-capped mountain tops are reflected in the warm Mediterranean. The most barren rocky tracts in the world, washed by Europe's most abundant rainfalls, are contiguous with an exotic littoral, magnificent lakes and the most luxuriant pastureland in the Balkans. The changes of scenery are so sudden that they almost seem miraculous. If creation is a miracle in itself, Montenegro is a miracle of creation.

Montenegro is a coastal, continental and mountainous country. It features four different climates, with many minor variations. High above the zone of contact between its subtropic and subpolar areas, northbound air streams from Africa meet southbound polar ones. There are forty lakes in Montenegro, and its rivers have remained Europe's purest thanks to the speed of their flow and to human care. Eighty percent of Montenegro is covered with forest, pasture and meadows. A total of 2,833 plant species and subspecies grow here. In other words, nearly a quarter of Europe's entire flora can be found on a mere 0.14 percent of the continent's territory. Four national parks and numerous beauty spots protected by law cover almost one-third of Montenegro. They provide shelter for its abundant flora and fauna, some of whose species cannot be found anywhere else in the world. Montenegro is also a land of natural rarities. It is home to one of Europe's only two jungles, the world's southernmost bay of glacial origin, the second deepest and longest river canyon and the longest underground river, the largest lake in the Balkans and the purest river in Europe.

The geography of Montenegro is inseparable from its history. Its amazing natural features have endowed the Montenegrins with their astounding ability to survive and defend their freedom in the harshest of conditions. In days of old while great empires were carving up Europe, by fire and sword, Montenegro found itself in the way of most of them. Its people fought in many wars, losing occasionally the most beautiful and richest parts of their country, and were forced to flee into inaccessible arid hills, but they were never vanquished. Squeezed between huge empires, the small and free Montenegro was a big problem for cartographers as it was impossible to write all the letters of its long name into the small space assigned to it on a map.

The interdependence of Montenegro's geography and its people may best be brought home by the following story from World War I. The powerful imperial army of Austria-Hungary constantly suffered defeats at the hands of the small but highly mobile Montenegrin army. Montenegrin soldiers seemed to mount their attacks out of nowhere, quickly disappearing into the countless gorges and ravines. In order to put an end to this practice, the Austrians ordered a huge relief map of Montenegro. Two-dimensional maps failed to reveal the true size of this apparently tiny country. What Montenegro lacked in length and width it made up for in depth and height. But not even the 3-D model of Montenegro on a scale of 1:10,000 was any good to the Austrians. The would-be conquerors were eventually gone, and to this day the model has remained a prime tourist attraction.

Despite his divine potential, man cannot replace the Creator. If the world was made in six days, it must have taken God 16.3 seconds to create Montenegro. Yet even in that fleeting interval the feelings of infinite mercy and capricious anger must have alternated in God's mind. The wrath of the Almighty seems to have sealed the fate of this territory and its people.

The book of Montenegro's creation could have been written in the following order.

The contrast between the serene beauty and charming
waters of the Adriatic and the brutal bare mountains of
Montenegro inspire fear. On the one hand the blue waters of the
bay, the most bewitching in Europe, the green fertile earth with the
gleam of small white towns set along the coast; and on the other
hand a sea of gloomy, bristling mountains with their
grey clouds, decorated only with small plots of cultivated land.
L. Asserin (c. 1933), French writer

The coast

To begin creating Montenegro in the south certainly made for a splendid introduction. The Adriatic is a warm sea, linked to the central Mediterranean by the Strait of Otranto. It is widest between Montenegro and southern Italy (about 200 km). This is also the deepest part of the Adriatic (1,330 m at a point 120 km southwest of Boka Kotorska Bay). The Montenegrin coast is washed by fresh currents bringing it the richness of marine life.

The coastline indentation ratio is about three: the full length of the coastline is 293.5 km, but only 90 km as the crow flies. With his mighty and generous hand, the Creator has dropped "sand jewels", 52 km of sand beaches, throughout the length of the coast. Almost every beach, like a vast arch, is the boundary of a small cove, sheltered from the wind and breakers. The 13-km-long beach in Ulcinj, in the southernmost part of Montenegro, has the finest sand imaginable. That in Bečići was declared Europe's most beautiful beach in 1930. And so all the way to Herceg Novi, a town on the border with Croatia.

Ulcinj, Bar, Petrovac, Budva, Tivat, Kotor and Herceg Novi have remained typical coastal towns. Modern urbanization has not destroyed their Mediterranean soul, enriched by a singular mixture of religions and cultures. The old well-preserved town centres are precious monuments of bygone days, but they are as much a part of everyday life as are the modern-day buildings. The ancient ramparts, towers, castles, monasteries, summer houses and royal residencies are not just museums but places where people still live and work.

The Montenegrin littoral is very narrow. It is separated from the hinterland by the steep karst mountains of Rumija (1,595 m), Sutorman (1,180 m), Orjen (1,895 m) and Lovćen (1,749 m). It is widest in the region of Boka Kotorska Bay (about 10 km) and narrowest at Paštrovići (less than 2 km). The coast is very rugged, but with hardly an island off it. There are many bays (Budva, Bar) and coves (Petrovac, Lučice, Buljarica, Čanj, Ulcinj), the most beautiful of them being Boka Kotorska Bay. Located between the Luštica and Prevlaka peninsulas, consisting of four smaller bays (Herceg Novi, Tivat, Risan and Kotor), crisscrossed by inlets and cutting deep into the mainland, it is one of Europe's most beautiful bays and the world's southernmost fjord. One is led to believe that it is the sea that flows into Boka Kotorska, forming a broad, highly ramified delta, rather than the other way round.

The Adriatic is one of the cleanest and most transparent seas, with abundant flora and fauna. Lemons, oranges and other Mediterranean and tropical fruits are grown on the coast. Large olive groves, some of whose trees are 2,000 years old, are a special attraction.

Montenegro has a rich tradition of seaside tourism. It boasts modern hotels, restaurants and accompanying facilities. The good roads, the Port of Bar (only 180 km from the Strait of Otranto), the numerous marinas and lagoons and the airports at Tivat and Podgorica all make this colourful area easily accessible to tourists from all over the world.

13.
Ulcinj - one of the tourist centres of Montenegro,
with numerous traces of a turbulent past

14-17.
Tourist resort of Ada Bojana, Ulcinj,
at the mouth of the Bojana

With his mighty and generous hand, the Creator has dropped "sand jewels", 52 km of sand beaches, throughout the length of the coast. The 13km long beach in Ulcinj, in the southernmost part of Montenegro, has the finest sand imaginable.

16

17

18.
"Kalimera" - wooden stand on water used by fishermen in Ulcinj
19.
Cape Djeran near Ulcinj

20.
Ulcinj - the southernmost city on the Montenegrin littoral
21.
A fierce clinch of the sea, sand and rock - a detail from the coast near Petrovac
22.
Cliff Katić near Petrovac

23-24.
Sveti Stefan has become a visual symbol of the Montenegrin tourism. In addition to the undoubtful "photogenic" qualities, this small peninsula is one of the most pleasant and picturesque places on the Montenegrin coast. Therefore the hotel-village of Sveti Stefan is the most exclusive item in the Montenegrin tourism's offer.

25.
The rough forecourt of paradise - a detail from the Budva riviera
26.
Budva - the Old Town citadel
27.
Jaz beach near Budva
28.
Budva-a combination of the past and modern times

29

29.
Old Town Budva, a medley of narrow paved streets and squares, with houses made of ashlar - all in a fine and natural harmony with the surrounding modern architecture and other features of a 20th-century city
30.
Budva fortifications - once a protection from enemies, today a witness of a centuries-long existence and a gazebo offering magic pictures to the eye

31.
The Bay of Tivat

32.
Thanks to its accessibility, in the distant past the Tivat Bay
was convenient for setting up of setllements whose inhabitants
were mostly fishermen and mariners

33

33.
Sveti Marko Island in the Bay of Tivat
34.
Herceg Novi - the northernmost city on the Montenegrin coast, more than 600 years old

34

35

35-36.
Sea sculptures in granite

64

The changes of scenery are so sudden that they almost seem miraculous. Snow-capped mountain tops are reflected in the warm Mediterranean. The most barren rocky tracts in the world are washed by Europe's most abundant rainfalls.

37.
Crkvice, above the Bay of Risan - the area with the highest rainfall rate in Europe
38.
The Bay of Risan

39-40.
Perast in Boka Kotorska
41.
Muo - a fishermen's village in Boka Kotorska

40

41

42.
The Bay of Kotor
43.
The ancient walls of Kotor - a part of the world's cultural heritage
44.
*Kotor: the serpentine path (foreground) leading to Cetinje
was once the only connection with the hinterland*

44

*... What attracted me was what I saw when I got there where the light of history is forged,
where the spirit and fantasy find their richest food, where life only half resembles reality
and more resembles a multifaceted fairy tale, if not a new edition of the
"Iliad".*

Jozef Holecek (1853 - 1939), Czech author and journalist

45

45.
Kotor: the romanesque cathedral of Sveti Tripun, 1166
46.
Kotor: "Trg od oružja" (Arms Square) with the
"Toranj" (Tower), 1602; the clock was made in early 19th century

The karst plateau

The Creator himself must have staggered at the beauty and abundance he had made on the coast and decided to protect it with impassable mountains apparently rising straight from the sea and for centuries presenting an insurmountable barrier to the people living beyond their peaks. Today good roads link the littoral to the hinterland, coiling like gigantic snakes round the steep slopes, just as narrow paths did in the past. The most famous of these serpentines are those in the Kotor and Petrovac areas. Beyond the mountains is a landscape of grey yet graphic limestone. Numerous limestone ridges rise from the tall and spacious karst plateau, full of funnel-shaped depressions and crevices and covered with "bare scattered stones giving the terrain the appearance of a heaving sea." This is Montenegro's second geomorphological region, the karst plateau. It is a beautiful sight to observe, but torture for the hands and souls of those living there. This moonscape is in stark contrast to the littoral it towers over. Its flora and fauna are sparse, a perfect example of the survival of the fittest. Shrubberies, copses and herbaceous plants are the only vegetation. Large mammals such as wolves and boars are very rare. Rabbits and foxes are more numerous, but it is reptiles that really feel at home here, with six different lizard species and six different snake species living in the karst. The avian population includes Greek partridges, thrushes and warblers.

Water passes through limestone easily, and not even abundant rainfalls can be of much help to the region. It is interesting to note that Krivošije, above Boka Kotorska Bay, has an average annual rainfall of 480 mm per sq m, which makes it the rainiest place in Europe. This is a tantalizing situation: plenty of rain and hardly any water for human consumption. Not far from there, in Ulcinj, the longest rainless period of eighty-one days has been recorded.

Amidst this barrenness lies Lovćen National Park, with its luxuriant forests and surreal vistas. Its perimeter is adorned with true gems: Boka Kotorska Bay, Lake Skadar, the Zeta and Bijelopavlići plains (Montenegro's largest fertile area) and the woods and pasture of Mts Golija, Vojnik and Prekornica. With Lovćen we end the story of the rough and dreary Montenegrin karst on a more cheerful note.

47.
Slopes of Mt. Lovćen (1,749 m)
48.
"The sea of rocks": a detail from the zone of vast rocklands

The valley of central Montenegro

The Creator decided that the next part of Montenegro should be far more suitable for human habitation. Lake Skadar and the fertile Zeta plains, with the Zeta river valley and Nikšić field, constitute Montenegro's third geomorphological area. This is the only large expanse of flat land in Montenegro.

The northern part of the Zeta plains lies about 40 m above sea level, while its Nikšić field lies 500 m higher. The rivers Morača, Ribnica and Cijevna also run through the lowlands.

49

Fertile river valleys always make ideal locations for human settlements. Population density in Montenegro is highest in the Zeta plains, which are home to Montenegro's two largest cities - the capital Podgorica and Nikšić.

A special adornment to the region is Lake Skadar National Park, the largest in the Balkans.

49.
The River Zeta valley in the central part of Montenegro
50.
Oboštinsko oko - the second spring of the Zeta reappearing after sinking

The high mountains

Mountains rise sharply yet elegantly from Montenegro's plains. If in the summer you drive northwards from Podgorica and its near-tropical temperatures of up to 40C by the road linking the Montenegrin coast with Serbia, it will take you only fifteen minutes to reach an area with a continental climate. Built decades ago, the road leads through Platije, the magnificent canyon of the Morača river. The dark mountain sides, like huge walls, meet high above the vehicles that to an observer on the edge of a cliff appear like barely visible, slow-moving dots. Alongside the road stretches an abyss in which the Morača river meanders like a silvery thread. One cannot help wondering how this narrow and shallow rivulet could have created such a vast chasm.

The northern part of Montenegro is an area of high limestone mountains. From a plateau lying about 1,700 m above sea level rise broad mountain ranges and ridges over 2,000 m high (Durmitor, Vojnik, Moračka kapa, Maganik). The rivers Piva, Tara, Morača, Ćehotina and their tributaries have cut deep and narrow beds with steep sides into the limestone - large canyons of unparalleled beauty.

The northeastern part of Montenegro is an area of sand and shale, also with many high mountains (Bjelasica, Komovi, Visitor) rich in pasture, forest and lakes. (There are twenty-nine mountain lakes in the whole of Montenegro.)

These are two separate regions in terms of geomorphology, but in all other respects they constitute a single whole. Two magnificent national parks, Biogradska Gora and Durmitor, are in this area.

The Tara is the longest mountain river in Montenegro (150 km). Its canyon, about 80 km long, cut between the mountains of Sinjajevina and Durmitor on one side and Ljubišnja and Zlatni Bor on the other, has an average depth of about 1,000 m. The canyon is 1,300 m deep near Obzir, which makes it the second deepest and longest canyon in the world, after the Grand Canyon of Colorado. The Tara canyon is a perfect example of wild pristine nature. For years, rafting down the Tara has been a great challenge for many an adventurer. Explorers are also attracted to the canyons cut by the rivers flowing into the Tara. The Sušica river canyon is about 15 km long and 600-800 m deep; the Vaškovska river canyon is about 2 km long, 1 km wide and about 700 m deep; the Draga river canyon is 7 km long and about 700 m deep.

The entire northern Montenegro is an oasis of undefiled nature. The industrial plants in Berane and Bijelo Polje, in the fertile valley of the Lim river, and those in Pljevlja, the northernmost town in Montenegro, have not done any serious damage to the environment. Montenegro's strategy in recent years has been to give priority to the production of health food and tourism and to use its vast natural resources more wisely and more economically.

52

51.
Stožina peak (1,668 m) on Mt. Durmitor
52 - 53.
Brnik peak on Mt. Lukavica
54.
Lake Manito on Mt. Lukavica

53

Alongside the Adriatic Sea amongst its brutal rock is found Montenegro. History glorifies this eagle's nest. This is an unconquerable homeland as glorious as Sparta. Her little nation is the only one of all the great Slavic races which has never been in the chains of slavery.

Gaston Rupnel (1871 - 1946), French writer

55-57.
"Katun" (a mountain summer pasture-land and shepherds' dwelling) on Zagarač, central Montenegro
58.
Lake Kapetanovo on Mt. Lukavica

Montenegrins are by nature and character as hard as their rocks.
Tall, well-built, of iron constitution; they have a warrior spirit,
which they instill from an early age, they develop unusual strength.
Francois Lenorman (1837 -1883), French scientist

59-60.
The Mrtvica canyon (near the Morača Monastery, between Podgorica-Kolašin)
with the road cut into its perpendicular side

61

62

63

61-64.
Flora in the Mrtvica canyon

65

65.
Čakor peak (2,046 m) on Mt. Prokletije
66.
Lake Ridsko on Mt. Prokletije - 1,970 m above the sea

66

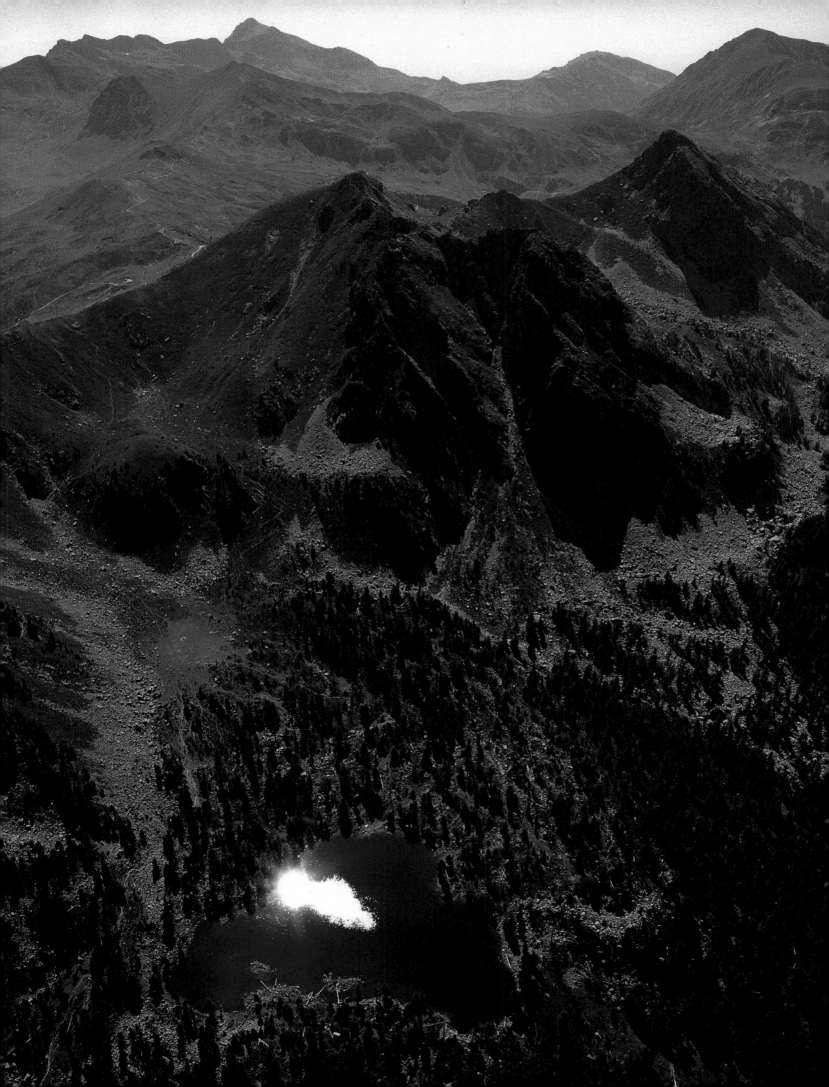

67.
The River Morača Canyon.

68.
The River Morača Canyon.

70

71

*It is not always a feat to jump
over a dizzily deep river gorge*

69-75.
Details from the Nevidio canyon, 3 km long, cut deep by the River Komarnica into the Durmitor karst. The sides of the canyon are at places only 2-3 metres apart. It is virtually inaccessible and was for the first time examined by alpinists from Nikšić in 1965. This mystic place abounds in cascades and falling waters of extreme beauty

76-77.
The Piva canyon

78-79.
Lake Trnovačko squeezed between
Mt. Maglić and Mt. Volujak

*This land can be proud of the wondrous beauty of its regions.Mountain
surpassing mountain and graceful wild valleys are its characteristic marks.*
H.F Winnington-Ingram (c. 1844), British Admiral

*International conventions, laws and urban-development
plans protect Montenegro's numerous national parks and
beauty spots, which cover twenty-eight percent
of its territory.
The city of Kotor was placed on UNESCO's endangered
world cultural heritage list in 1979, Kotor-Risan Bay on
UNESCO's world cultural heritage list in the same year,
and Durmitor National Park on UNESCO's natural
heritage list in 1980. The Tara river basin became part of
UNESCO's Man and Biosphere (MAB)
programme in 1977.
Montenegro's Environmental Protection Act
applies to monuments of nature, such as canyons and
gorges, natural preserves (plant and animal habitats),
beaches, man-modified natural objects and other natural
objects whose protection is considered to be in the interests of the state.
A special decision by Montenegro's Institute for Environmental Protection ensures special care for 52 plant and
314 animal species in Montenegro, including all
of its bat species.*

*80.
Lake Crno on Mt. Durmitor at 1,422 m above the sea*

NATIONAL PARKS

Lovćen National Park

With a total area of 6,400 ha, Lovćen National Park is more important for its cultural and historical sites than for the beauty of its nature. The park is dominated by Mt Lovćen, on top of which stands a mausoleum dedicated to Petar Petrović Njegoš, Montenegro's great 19th-century poet-philosopher and spiritual and secular ruler.

Mt Lovćen is often referred to as "the Montenegrin Olympus". But whereas people once believed that anthropomorphic gods lived on Mt Olympus, Mt Lovćen has been hallowed by real men's spiritual, artistic and military achievements. For centuries it was the retreat of Montenegrin rulers. The first South Slavic book in Cyrillic script was printed here in 1494. This

81

was the only place between the Turkish and Austrian-Hungarian empires marked on maps with a special colour signifying free territory. Cetinje, Montenegro's old capital and a museum of Montenegrin history, is also part of Lovćen National Park.

But the park is not without natural attractions. It covers a typically Mediterranean area, an Alpine zone and marshes close to Lake Skadar.

The climatic and geographic variety of Lovćen National Park is paralleled by the diversity of its flora and fauna.

81.
"Katun" on Mt. Lovćen
82.
*Mausoleum on Mt. Lovćen - the monument to Petar II Petrović Njegoš (Nyegosh),
Montenegrin Prince-Bishop and great poet and philosopher (19th c.)*

83.
Mt. Lovćen (1,749 m) in the southern part of Montenegro - a symbol of Montenegrin spirituality and state-
hood, at the foot of which lies Cetinje that has been the capital of Montenegro for centuries
84.
Ceklin - an area near Cetinje

85

86

87.
Present-day Cetinje

88

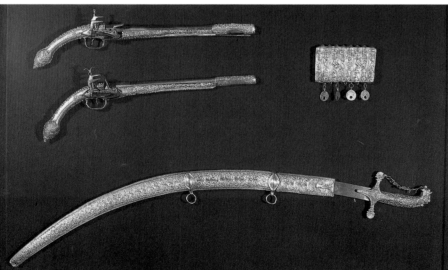

89

91.
State Museum in Cetinje (former Government building)
92.
Ceremonial hand-arms of King Nikola
collections of State Museum in Cetinje

90

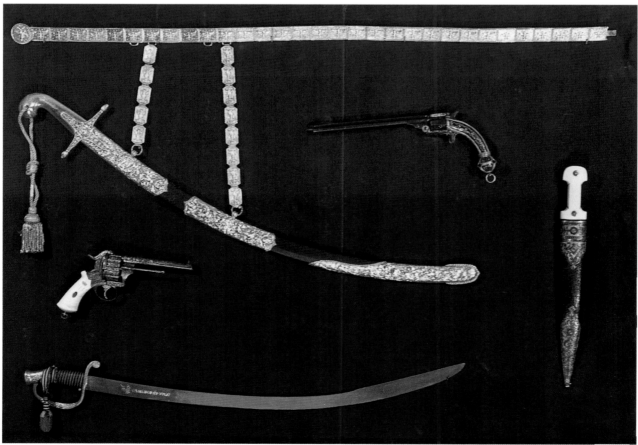

Lake Skadar National Park

Lake Skadar is over 40 km long and has an average width of about 10 km. When its water level is low, it covers an area of some 370 km^2. After abundant spring and autumn rainfalls, the lake covers 530 km^2. It is the largest lake in the Balkans and geologically the youngest lake in Europe. Two-thirds of it belong to Montenegro, and one-third to Albania.

It is mostly shallow but is up to 44 m deep in places. As the lake is 6 m above sea level during periods of average water levels, its bottom lies 38 m below sea level at its lowest. Lake Skadar is a typical cryptodepression, the largest and most distinct one in the Balkans.

Lake Skadar was declared a national park in 1983. The park covers an area of 40,000 ha, and its valley is separated from the sea by 7 km wide Mt Rumija.

Its main asset is its plentiful flora and fauna. More than 40 fish species live in it, some of which - like bleak and trout species - cannot be found anywhere else in the world. For centuries the most important economic activities of the people living on Lake Skadar's shore have been fishing and the cultivation of the fertile soil left after the withdrawal of the flood.

There are 270 different bird species in Lake Skadar National Park. The best known is the pelican, which has found here its last refuge in Europe and is in a sense the hallmark of the lake.

The flora is rich and varied. Apart from the colourful swamp plants, the rare water chestnut and carnivorous plants are also very interesting. Yellow water lilies sometimes cover the waters close to the shore so densely that observers have the impression of looking at vast mountain meadows.

As anywhere else in Montenegro, the lake's shore, promontories and numerous uninhabited islets hide remnants of a stormy past. One meets history at every step one takes. Particularly interesting are Žabljak, a splendid fort and the capital of Zeta during the Crnojević era, built in 1478, 44 m long and 25 m wide and encircled by walls 14 m tall and 2 m thick; Lesendro, an imposing fort erected on a bare rock rising from the sea; Grmožur fort, on a stone islet not far from Lesendro, built by the Turks after 1843.

Finally, numerous fresh water springs gush from the bottom of the lake, making it an inexhaustible source of potable water.

93-99.
Motifs from Lake Skadar

98

*From the crest of the highest mountain range we had a wide view of
Lake Skadar... a truly bewitching panorama.*
Edward Ledwich Mitford (c. 1839)
English scientist and travel writer

100.
Lake Skadar
101.
Lake Skadar - a reservation of waterfowl
102.
Mt. Rumija divides Lake Skadar and the Adriatic Sea

100

101

103.
Umac near Virpazar
104.
Northwest banks of Lake Skadar grooved by numerous
small inlets, defiles and bays of exceptional beauty

105

106

105-107.
Details from Rijeka Crnojevića - a small town on the banks of Lake Skadar

108

109

108.
Ruins of old citadels are found on numerous isles in Lake Skadar
109.
The Beška Monastery - the Church of Holy Mother - on Beška Island in Lake Skadar
110.
Žabljak Crnojevića - a historic place on the banks of Lake Skadar: at high waters this fortified village becomes an island
111.
Lake Skadar - an abundance of flora and fauna

National Park Biogradska Gora

Biogradska Gora National Park, with an area of 5,400 ha, is unique in many ways. It is one of the only two jungles in Europe. (The other one is Perućica in Bosnia.) This precious preserve also enjoyed the protection of Montenegro's princes of old. It is believed than not a single tree has ever been cut down in Biogradska Gora.

Over 80 tree species grow in this jungle. Some of the fir trees are up to 50 m tall, and the acers and birches are only slightly smaller. The national park is also rich in animal life, with many different bird species and plenty of big and small game. Man's constant efforts to preserve this ecological system have been very fruitful. Deer, roe deer and other animals move freely about, without any fear of man.

Lake Biograd lies in the very centre of Biogradska Gora. The lake side is well-groomed and easily accessible and is increasingly attracting Yugoslav and foreign tourists.

Man's early care for Biogradska gora can be regarded as the harbinger of what was to crystallize later as the idea of an Ecological State.

114

115

112.
Nature-made sculptures
in Biogradska Gora
National Park
113-115.
Lake Biogradsko
on Mt. Bjelasica - the centre
of Biogradska Gora
National Park
116.
A detail from the banks
of Lake Biogradsko

116

117

118

119

120

117.
A countrywoman in a Mt. Bjelasica "katun"
118.
Lake Biogradsko
119.
Mt. Bjelasica
120-121.
Pešića lake and Ursulovačko lake on Mt. Bjelasica

Durmitor National Park

Durmitor National Park is located in the region of the old Montenegrin mountains, in the country's far north, sprawling over 39,000 ha. Apart from the massive Mt Durmitor, it includes Jezera plateau, the Piva mountains, the Sušica canyon and part of the Tara canyon. Part of this national park and the Tara canyon were placed on UNESCO's world heritage list in 1980. The section of the national park belonging to the Tara watershed has been protected as part of a network of international biosphere preserves.

Almost the entire Mt Durmitor is an oasis of pasture and vast forests. The mountain's special attractions are its 19 blue lakes called "mountain eyes", some of them lying at altitudes higher than 2,000 m. Durmitor's lowest point, the confluence of the Piva and Tara rivers, is 433 m above sea level, and its highest point and the highest peak in Montenegro, called Bobotov Kuk, is 2,523 m above sea level. The town of Žabljak, the centre of Montenegro's winter tourism, is also located on Mt Durmitor.

122

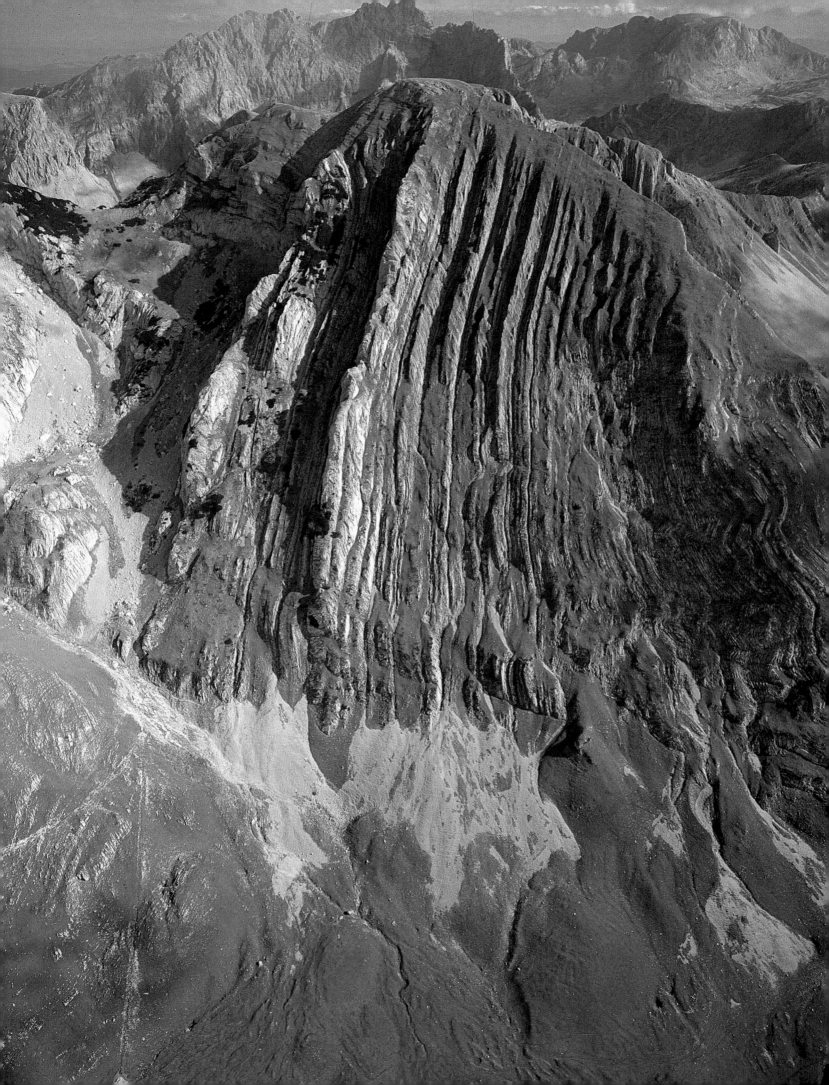

125

122.
Dobri Do "katun" on Mt. Durmitor
123.
Prutaš peak (2,393 m) on Mt. Durmitor
124.
The Durmitor massif has 22 peaks over 2,200 m in height

150

125.
The Škrka canyon on Mt. Durmitor
126.
Mt. Durmitor: Lake Škrčko, and Bobotov Kuk - the highest peak in Montenegro (2,523 m)
127.
A view of Durmitor from Žabljak, the largest place Mt. Durmitor and centre of winter tourism

128

128.
"Stećak" (tombstone) on Mt. Durmitor
129.
Mt. Durmitor: the Skakala waterfall

*Amongst these mountains open up panoramas which can
look like the realization of the most
fantastic romantic or historical description.*
Sir John Gardner Wilkinson (1797 - 1875)
British archaeologist

130

131

130.
Mt.Durmitor
131.
"Ledena pećina" (The Ice Cave) on Mt. Durmitor - one of 200 caves surveyed in the area
132.
Mt. Durmitor: a view from the peak Prutaš (2,393 m)

133-137.
Stožina peak (1,668 m) on Mt. Durmitor: living with its sunrises and sunsets, its seasons, rains and storms it always offers a different appearance

138

138-140.
Mt. Durmitor in its winter attire - a challenge for alpinists, a paradise for winter sports fans,
and a realm of wonderful landscapes testifying that long lasting snow and ice must not always
offer a bleak and harsh picture

141.
A waterfall on the River Tušinja

142.
The Skakavica waterfall
in the Komarnica valley
143.
Mt. Durmitor: winter games
of nature in the
Komarsko region
(below the Savin Kuk peak)

144

147

147.
Lake Pošćensko on Mt. Durmitor
148.
A detail from Mt. Sinjajevina
149.
The Komarnica valley with Boljska Greda

148

149

150.
Mt. Durmitor: the Sušica canyon

151.
Mt. Durmitor: lakes Barno and Crno

152.
Lake Zminje
153.
The Čelina Waterfall on Mt. Durmitor

154

155

156

154.
Pošćenska valley
155-156.
Todorov Do

157

157-158.
The Tara canyon: by its length (80 km) and depth (1,300 m) it is the world's second largest canyon after the
Grand Canyon of Colorado (USA)

159

159.
Durmitor National Park: a large reservation of the rare species of dark pine
(**pinus nigra**) *covers the rocky terraces of Crna Poda*
160.
The lower course of the Tara - a raftsmen's realm

161.
The village of Aluge at the turn of autumn into winter

162.
Mt. Durmitor's winter adornments

181

163-165.
The mouth of the River Ljutica (flowing into the Tara)

166.
Lake Zabojsko
167-168.
In the Tara canyon

167

168

169-170.
Kayakers and rafters on the Tara

Over the centuries,
Montenegrins have developed
the notion that all cultural and religious
monuments, even those created by
one-time enemies, deserve respect
and attention, even though these
were the product of temporary or centuries
long enemies. Having the feeling of respect for
themselves and their convictions,
Montenegrins have felt the same towards
everyone else.

171.
"Stećci" (tombstones) on Mt. Durmitor

HISTORY

The history of Montenegro is one of a constant struggle for freedom and an independent state. Its border regions over the centuries more resembled army camps than dwelling places. Montenegrin children learned to grow up without their fathers, to whom the responsibility to fight for the freedom and survival of their country was more important than looking after their family and personal happiness.

Montenegrins not only created their own history, they rescued it from oblivion. At first by oral transmission from generation to generation, and then in books. The book has even nowadays almost a magical power in Montenegro. Whether written by hand or printed on the first state printing press in the world, the book was the weapon for defending historical identity and the spirit of freedom. Even at a time when only a small minority were literate, over five hundred years ago, Montenegrin rulers knew that war was waged not only with the sword but that the pen could be equally powerful.

The history of Montenegro, because of constant war, poverty and the lack of well-educated people, abounds in events that more resemble romantic national enthusiasm than scientifically confirmed facts. But this is in no way unusual. Besides which, which people in its memories and legends talks about its weaknesses and mistakes? The epic and idyllic picture of Montenegrin history has been strengthened by numerous romantically spirited visitors to Montenegro. Many contributions, especially towards the end of the last century, informed Europe that Montenegro was the new "Sparta", or the "stone throne of liberty". The main motif underlying this praise was a sincere respect and love for a small and freedom-loving people. But neither should we neglect the desire of those writers to stimulate a similar feeling in the countries from which they came by praising the fighting spirit and glorious victories of Montenegro.

On the other hand Montenegro, surrounded by numerous strong enemies, was often strongly criticized by those to whom a strong Montenegro was not in their interest. Thus false propaganda was spread, many insulting claims were made and everything for which Montenegro stood proud was negated. Some opined that it was impossible for such a small and weak state to defy the mighty kingdoms, so that its freedom and independence were just a farce hiding the real situation. In this way a state that had endured so much in order not to suffer slavery, now had this very same freedom challenged, a freedom it had achieved with great difficulty and with much bitter fruit.

However objective analysts, on whose judgment modern historical science is based, are one in their evaluation. Montenegrin history is above all one of a constant struggle against all those who attack its freedom, and revenge on all those who decide to cross its borders. Often the enemy was not only incomparably stronger, but also in alliance with others. Cruel reality demanded a choice between two evils. Thus on occasions treaties were made which meant obligations towards protectors, allies and enemies. There were cases when some tribes temporarily recognised the sovereignty of others. Thus on occasions treaties were made which meant obligations towards protectors, allies and enemies. There were cases when some tribes temporarily recognised the sovereignty of others, subjugating themselves to the more powerful. This was always an expression of necessity and actually a means of protecting true independence. As soon as they got back to modest strength and the general climate at all allowed it they would return to the normal situation. Montenegro mainly followed Russian political interests because of their common Slav origins, primordial friendship and shared faith. The Montenegrin philosophy is summed up in one document, "we don't wish to have a subject relationship with another, and we will protect the freedom which our ancestors willed us - to the last, ready rather to die with sword in hand than to become the slaves of whatever country".

This message reached other friendly states. Messages sent to other addresses were not only in words but in heroic acts which were finally recognised and weighed up by the whole civilised world. Europe recognised the results of the Montenegrin people's enduring and unstinting struggle at the end of the twentieth century, accepting it into its ranks, and thus affirming its contribution to the culture and civilisation of the old continent.

CENTURIES OF STRUGGLE FOR STATEHOOD

172

Montenegro has its historical roots in the 7th century, with the arrival of the Slavs in the Balkan peninsula. All traces of the previous population and their state organisation have disappeared from the consciousness of the nation and there are no written documents. Archaeological remains, which because of the general conditions existing throughout the ages have never been properly examined, give only a faint hint of the far past.

Very early on there was a strong Hellenistic influence in this area on civilisation and culture. The Adriatic coast, geographically close and known to skillful Greek sailors, was a route for the spread of powerful empires, firstly Greek and then Roman. The Illyrians, the original inhabitants of this region, with time merged into their state organisations.

Modern Montenegro covers a very similar area to the Roman region of Doclea. Administratively it belonged to Illyria, that is to say Eastern Illyrica. In the 6th century Emperor Justinian established Byzantine rulership over the whole Balkan peninsula right to the Adriatic Sea.

Unable to defend themselves against the attacks of the Barbarian tribes, especially the Avars, the weakened empire called on the Slavs to help. They were obviously already known to the Byzantines. They were clearly sufficiently cultured to communicate with little problem with their own population, but also sufficiently strong to throw back the destructive onslaughts of Avars. The Avars were resisted, and the Slavs peacefully immigrated and were well received. Very quickly they became Christians.

The division of Christianity in the mid of the 11th century into the Roman Catholic and Orthodox churches left a long impression on the then Zeta. Zeta was thus the third name for today's Montenegro, a name which long represented this region. Thus Zeta was established at the crossing of Rome and Byzantinum, and was forced by necessity to learn to live between two opposite worlds. The double influence had to be neutralised since otherwise survival was impossible. Thus Zeta cleared a path for its own cultural journey.

Thanks to its geographical location Zeta and its districts had no rivals amongst its neighbours, despite them having larger and richer territories at their disposal. Zeta was a small, but complete whole. It was able to act independently, to expand on all sides, but whilst doing so not to be at great risk. It was out of Zeta itself that the great Serbian districts grew, which eventually united all Serbian lands under one imperial crown.

The rulers of Zeta were always among the strongest district rulers. At the beginning of the 11th century Vladimir, the ruler of Zeta, was called King. In the second half of the same century Pope Gregory VII gave Mihailo, the ruler of Zeta, the title Serbian King. After thirty years of his reign the Greeks temporarily subjugated Zeta. Behind all this on the historical scene stands the Serbian state, which didn't only include Zeta, but also an important part of the Byzantine Empire.

The ruling family Nemanjić experienced its greatest ascent at the time of the Emperor Dušan, who by dint of good organisation and brilliant war victories succeeded in arriving at the gates of the Byzantine Empire with the intention of taking that throne. He died before his intention was achieved, and quickly following his demise his powerful empire also fell. The fault wasn't so much with his insufficiently capable successors, but more in the fact that the growth of the Turkish tribes was beginning already to threaten Europe, a threat which would cast a dark shadow over the following centuries. Dušan's empire burst at the seams. The small and internally discordant states couldn't offer much defense against the Turkish onslaught from Asia. When the whole of the Balkan peninsula had been subdued by the Turks, and when no-one from Western Europe had raised arms against Turkish power, the leaders of Zeta unfurled their battle flag and for a whole one hundred years after the fall of the Serbian Empire defended their independence, giving way only step by step. It could be said that this was a kind of debt to the Nemanjićs who were born in Zeta, who saw Zeta as their own by birth, and which served them in achieving wide political aims.

For the following seventy years or so Zeta was led by the Balšić dynasty. Threatened by the Turkish onslaught they were forced to improve their relationship with another powerful neighbour, Venice. They gave Venice full and free trading rights, and in return had the right to be called Venetian citizens and sometimes to be aided in struggles against the Turks.

Zeta was led by the Crnojevićs from 1427 to 1498. They attempted to keep the identity of Zeta as a separate state at the crossroads between the opposing powerful interests of Venice and the Turks. Right at the commencement of his rulership Stefan Crnojević recognised Venetian sovereignty, and together with the Venetians warred against the neighbouring Serbian despots, justifying this with the need to be protected against Turkish invasion. The Crnojevićs' primary place in Zeta political life was ensured by this recognition of Venice.

173

172.
*The Montenegrin flag from the battle of Vučji Do (1876) pierced by more than a hundred bullets;
collections of State Museum in Cetinje*
173.
Risan: a Roman mosaic (3rd c.) depicting Hypnos, the God of Sleep

Side by side with the strengthening and increasing political confidence of the Crnojevićs the name of the great mountain massif Montenegro (Black Mountain) began to be seen as the motherland of the Crnojevićs. From ancient times they had controlled Mt Lovćen, the geographical and spiritual Olympus of Montenegro. The current name of the state which had changed so much, had entered into life. A name which would remain the same through the centuries in the face of many temptations.

Stefan's son Ivan Crnojević didn't base his politics on enmity with Turks and faithfulness to Venice. He calculatedly went in both directions, seeking thus to gain a greater degree of independence and political freedom. Nevertheless at the time of the great Turkish offensive (1479) he lost his country and found safety in Italy. Ivan returned three years later, at a time of great merciless dynastic in-fighting in the Turkish palace. It is not known how nor with whose aid, but by a surprise attack he managed to regain control of his old region and drive out the few representatives of Turkish control. Despite winning the battle against the Turkish troops, and without hope of Venetian aid, Ivan Crnojević had no choice but to approach the sultan offering him loyalty and probably paying tribute. Whilst in contacts with the outside world the ruler of Zeta had his hands tied, at least within his own borders he was now independent.

Thus Montenegro became the last oasis of the once great Serbian empire at the end of the 15th century. In it the last flicker of state independence of the dismantled feudal Nemanjić state was slowly being extinguished. Within its internal life the rules of the old empire were still kept and recognised. The spiritual culture of the Orthodox East were nurtured, implanted in the consciousness and traditions of the people, but also protected by state concern and influence.

174

The Serbian Orthodox Church was forced to reduce its activities. Turkish campaigns and the destruction of churches and monasteries on the one hand, and the efforts of the Roman Catholic Church to strengthen its position on the other forced the Zeta Metropolitan deeper into the safety of the mountains. In 1485 the seat of

174.
The heraldic
bearnigs of
Ivan Crnojević
the ruler of Zeta
(former name of
Montenegro)
1465-1490

the Metropolitan was moved to Cetinje, where a church and monastery dedicated to the Virgin Mary were built. All of this of course was done with the help of the Crnojevićs. Ivan's son Djurdje dedicated his time and energy to religous books as a method of protecting the faith and the national identity. The first cyrillic printing press in Slavic southern Europe, and the first state printing press, was founded as a result of this. Thus the state was saved by books. What the force of arms couldn't acheive was done by Gutenberg's press.

For the nation to survive in a spiritual, and even in a physical sense, it was necessary to unite bravery, moral endurance, national commitment, and the orthodox faith.

Numerous limestone ridges rise from the tall and spacious karst plateau,
full of funnel - shaped depressions and crevices and covered with "bare scattered stones
giving the terrain the appearance of a heaving sea." It is a beautiful sight to observe, but
torture for the hands and souls of those living there.

175-176.
Rijeka Crnojevića
177.
Tke Gulf of Kotor (Boka Kotorska)

THE PETROVIĆ - NJEGOŠ DYNASTY

Ivan Crnojević transferred his capital to Cetinje. He took with him the Metropolitan of the Orthodox Church whom he considered equal to him in rank. Although he was still called the "ruler of Zeta" this was the beginning of the history of Montenegro.

At that time the Turks had conquered all the lands of the former Serbian Empire. Freedom was defended by a handful of people around Crnojević and the church. With unlimited bravery, and although somewhat protected by the mountains, they still realised that their prospects were slim. Ivan Crnojević made a far reaching decision. In his new capital he built a monastery and church rather than a palace. He invested without complaint his last material possessions in the raising of beautiful religious buildings. He knew that he couldn't raise the state's military power to the necessary level. Thus he favoured the spiritual power of his nation which he believed to be indestructible in its ideals and moral principles, and which the Orthodox church alone at that time could nurture.

When finally his son Djurdje left Montenegro, the nation was left alone with its spiritual leader. His church jurisdiction spread over the whole region of former Zeta and was a symbolic reminder of the power of the former state. Thus was faith in a better day increased and strength gathered for the every day clashes with the powerful and arrogant encircling enemy.

With the departure of the Crnojevićs the state organisation disappeared and the nation was returned to tribal and family divisions. Powerful and rich families were at the head of these tribes. They often thought no further than personal interest, or the strengthening of their own family unit. Thus conflicts between tribes became more and more frequent, which added to the weakening of the nation and decreased its modest strength. The one element of unity was to be found in the Metropolitan, that is in the Bishop, as the people called him. But that this was insufficient is shown by the fact that the internal conflicts which the Bishops tried to prevent didn't stop for almost four hundred years. The Bishops had no real power, and prayer and anathemas had no influence on the arrogant and uneducated tribal leaders.

In these conditions a theocracy was formed in Montenegro. The Bishops were the first people of the state, but for a long time they had no way of accomplishing their desire to lead for the good of the state.

There are two periods in the Metropolitan leadership of Montenegro. In the first period, lasting almost two centuries, the title of leader belonged to people from various families. History numbers 15 Bishops. On average they lasted about 12 years in that function. In the second period the Bishop was chosen from the Petrović family, which represented the founding of a dynasty in Montenegro. In a period of 154 years there were 5 Bishops. Seeing as at one time there were two Bishops, on average each of them were in office almost 40 years.

However to be in power in a small, poor country, abandoned by all, and pressured by all, and alongside all this to rule without any opportunities wasn't exactly a privilege! Only the most gifted people freed of temptations in terms of gaining worldly wealth and position, and completely spiritually devoted to a very powerful idea and vision could do this. Only those who shared its fate - monks - could lead a nation which had been led to the edge of despair and pushed into absolute poverty. Because of this and in spite of their mistakes, real or invented faults, and the evaluations of those who came after them, each of them deserves admiration. Today it's difficult to understand how much they accomplished and how difficult it was to carry the burden entrusted to them.

Powerful Turkish armies from that time constantly pressured Montenegro. Every Montenegrin victory was at a high price. On the other hand it succeeded in enraging a many times stronger enemy. In 1690 the Skadar Suleiman-pasha broke through into Cetinje and burnt down the monastery raised by Ivan Crnojević. But even such a powerful army didn't have the strength to remain in Cetinje, but rather withdrew quickly leaving behind ruins. Cetinje was devastated in 1714 and 1785. Not a single Balkan country was attacked so much which says a lot for the size of the opposition to the Turks.

Clearly it was possible to defeat Montenegro, but not to hold it in subjugation.

178.
The Cetinje
Monastery
(built in 1484)

Bishop Danilo

Right at the time of defeat and despair, the national choice for the new Bishop was Danilo, the first from the Petrović household. His secular name was Nikola Petrović Šćepčević and he was a remarkable man. At the time when he accepted this spiritual responsibility he was only 16 years old. His contribution to Montenegrin history is especially remembered for two things. Firstly, because he forged relations with Russia, and thus introduced Montenegro into international politics. Secondly, because he organised the annihilation of local converts to Islam.

These converts recognised no rule but that of Turkey and openly worked for the breaking of all opposition to Turkish attacks. They represented a "state within a state". Because of this the Montenegrin assembly unanimously accepted Danilo's suggestion to deal with them finally. This measure was brutal, but carried out because absolutely necessary. This Montenegrin "night of the long knives" was carried out just before Christmas 1707. Some were killed and some were returned to their old faith, and thus had their lives saved - very quickly there were no converts to Islam left in Montenegro. However this was not the suffering of the harmless but actually a hard battle, many of the converts being well armed. This aspect of Montenegrin history has entered into mythology, above all else through the unfading work 'The Mountain Wreath' written by the greatest Montenegrin poet Bishop Peter II Petrović Njegoš. It is still true today that this book was written "from the mind of the whole nation", seeing as the Montenegrin who doesn't know at least some of it by heart is vary rare.

179. "Vladika" (Prince-Bishop) Danilo (author: Milo Vrbica, 1912); collections of State Museum in Cetinje

Very soon the long awaited message reached Montenegro. A strengthened Russia, led by Peter the Great, was calling Montenegro to a joint struggle against the Turks. The invitation was accepted with an enthusiasm hard to imagine. From then on within this relationship with Russia, which would decisively affect the position and fate of Montenegro, there was much joy and sorrow, hope and disappointment, all awoken in this small nation by the political stance of a powerful, beloved, but all too distant state-brotherly protector. Led by this initial fervour, the Montenegrins achieved a victory against the Turks at Carev Laz, which is considered to be the most significant victory of their arms and courage.

Bishop Danilo quickly travelled to Russia. Overwhelmed by the reception he received from Peter the Great he returned to Montenegro with tales that spread joy everywhere and created a new strength throughout the nation. Whatever the reality of the Russian backing it was the first support the Montenegrins had got for a very long time. From then on Montenegro was afraid of no risk and took every opportunity to fight the Turks.

His success at the Russian palace significantly increased the prestige and authority of Bishop Danilo. He exploited this to strengthen his power above tribal divisions.

Bishop Sava

The Bishop had the authority to name his successor, but the national assembly could veto his decision. Sava became the next Metropolitan. Historians sharply criticize his ability to run the state and this is corroborated by the fact that the people demanded he appointed a co-leader. The new Bishop Vasilije was given the task of running public affairs, and Sava went off to a monastery to take care of church matters.

Bishop Vasilije

Bishop Vasilije spent a large amount of his reign in Russia. His aim and ideal was the creation of a state which would oppose internal disorder and dissension between Montenegrin tribes and which would overcome corrupt and irresponsible tribal leaders. He realised that on his own he had neither the power nor the means to achieve this great aim, and he saw the power as coming from Russia. But Russia clearly didn't see it as its responsibility to help Montenegro except at times of joint wars. While on just such an attempt to receive help Vasilije died. His departure was particularly welcomed by Montenegro's enemies, the strongest of whom was Venice, in the justified belief that closeness to Russia would imperil its own interests with regard to Montenegro. Misunderstood and unhappy abroad, unsuccessful at home with his plan for Montenegro, he left his country in a difficult situation.

Yet again Montenegro returned to the will of the tribal leaders. Disunity reigned in which Montenegro was prevented from reacting to significant events taking place around it.

This internal situation favoured a historical episode an example of which it is difficult to find in other nations - the appearance of a false king, self-proclaimed and adventurer, who took the Montenegrin throne and whom the people named Šćepan the Small.

The unsubmissive and untamed nation chose an ignoramus for their king, believing him to be the dethroned and miraculously survived Russian Tzar Petar III. Not even the strongest army of the time could subject the Montenegrins and force them to follow foreign leadership. But what was impossible with the sword was achieved by illusion, love and faith in Russia. The reign of the false king, which lasted 7 years, at least had a positive result. In fact it was this reign that laid the foundation for the Montenegrin state movement. He succeeded in almost irradicating blood feuds, tribal frictions, violence, robbery and unpunished murder. Probably the Montenegrins found out very soon that his claims about himself were false, but in the current times and circumstances his mission seemed absolutely necessary. In support of this claim is his murder carried out at the orders of the Venetian Republic. Venice had long realised that those who worked for the strengthening of little Montenegro were dangerous to it and didn't hold back from using whatever methods were possible to remove these sort of people. Finally and just before his awful murder, Montenegrins respected the achievements of Šćepan the Small, rising above the temptation to get revenge on him for his deceit.

Petar the First

Quickly following this, one of the greatest and most important Montenegrin leaders ascended to the throne - Petar I. He was Bishop almost fifty years. No one before, nor happily after, endured such insults and suffering, fruitless effort and major disappointments. But no one but him remained as faithful in expending their last ounce of strength for their life ideal and persevering along the torturous road of the struggle for national advancement and well-being.

Petar I dedicated his whole life to uniting the quarrelling tribes and creating the organs of state power. He untiringly continued to create conditions for order and justice, and also to stop the conflicts which spent the people's energies and led to misfortune in relationships with enemies. The basis of every state is a tax system which pays for its servants. But the Montenegrins long refused to pay anyone, even their own state. The logic was - "when we already don't pay taxes to the Turks, and consequently we're always at war, why would we pay taxes to distant Cetinje when it cannot give us any sort of protection". The price of this was high.

Taking advantage of Bishop's absence and dissension amongst the tribes, the Turks destroyed Cetinje, all Montenegro and the coast in 1785. Afterwards he spent over a year walking amongst the people - giving advice, encouraging and restoring the national spirit.

Lacking means other than prayer and anathemas, Petar I constantly visited the quarreling tribes. He made peace, he swore oaths all in the aim of unity, oneness and justice. Because of his great authority the people grew to believe that those who disobeyed him would face the Bishop's damnation, which would sooner or later arrive. Many examples of the supernatural power of Petar I have entered into legend. Firstly the people and then the church considered him a saint. However it must be nearer the truth that the myth arose after his death, which truly united all Montenegro over his bier. Since if this had not been the case it would not have been necessary for him to spend all his life solving inter-personal conflicts.

There were dramatic failures in his activities. These didn't depend on his efforts but rather resulted from the general circumstances, primarily from the interests of the powerful states surrounding Montenegro. Thus Montenegro, at the call of Russia, Austria and England fought Napoleon, who was already the master of Europe. Montenegro became an active player in world events, and took on the tasks which history gave it with honour. Completely spent by the efforts of fighting France for 7 years, Montenegro, although a victor, was humiliated and forgotten at the Congress of Vienna, which took away its rights to spread its borders and to have an exit on the coast. The government lost its authority amongst the people and the currents of self-will and revolt took over. However not this, nor any other of the numerous problems, especially those in relation to Russia, could defeat Bishop Petar I.

180. Metropolitan Petar I Petrović (author: Ljubo Brajović); collections of the Montenegrin History Museum in Cetinje

In these circumstances it was impossible to expect progress in the areas of culture and education. His plans to stop the cultural slide backwards had to be left to those who would come later, and he himself was very unhappy about the poor circumstances in which his people lived and the rough habits which were forced on the nation by the times.

However Bishop Petar I achieved an incredible amount. He created national unity in the face of outside enemies. At his call Montenegro as one had risen to defend their homeland at the call of, "For the honourable cross and for golden freedom". Thus he de facto created all necessary preconditions for Montenegro to replace its spiritual leadership with a more solid form of state, monarchical rule. Due to him Montenegro received its first legal code in 1798.

Petar II Petrović Njegoš

Petar II Petrović Njegoš became the new Bishop. With the mind of a genius and artistically gifted, added to exceptional abilities for a philosophical understanding of the world, he leant towards poetry and had a thirst for knowledge, taken together he wasn't really born for the role of a spiritual leader. He became Bishop when he was 18, against his own will. However alongside the fact that he grew into one of the great world known poets, he proved himself to be an exceptional statesman.

Under his leadership Montenegro founded proper state institutions for the first time. A senate was set up, put together under the principle of tribal representation; an administrative body was created - the "Kapetan"; a "guard" was formed as the executive to oversee the carrying out of the government's decisions. A small tax was introduced which alongside Russian donations enabled the state apparatus to survive. The Bishop thus became a man in whose hands power was concentrated.

Instead of the until then worst punishment - exile - the death penalty was introduced, used sometimes on a large scale. The people were forced into obedience and learnt a fear that they hadn't known existed previously. This was completely in accordance with European states of the time. The basic principle of a monarchy was, and remains, to keep the people in fear and subjugation. Montenegrins submitted to these measures and grew accustomed to them, evaluating them as a lesser evil than the chaotic state which had existed for all too long in that region.

Njegoš opened the first school in Montenegro in 1834. The following year he symbolically renewed the work of the Crnojević's publishing house. However as much as he tried he

181. Petar II Petrović Njegoš (author: J.Tominc); collections of Njegoš's Museum in Cetinje

couldn't stimulate advances in cultural life. There were still constant wars with the Turks. The school was closed, and the lead letters of the press were converted into rifle bullets, in the time of Prince Danilo.

The then Europe was amazed at the struggle of the Montenegrins, but they didn't officially recognise Montenegro as an independent state. One of the reasons for this was the very unusual form of government of a spiritual leader in a secular role. Alongside the constant intrigues around Montenegro and its leader this was one of the reasons why the transfer to secular, autocratic rule was speeded up.

It is assumed that Njegoš couldn't see himself in the role of a secular leader from his moral principles. Alongside this a serious illness attacked his body and early ended his life in this world. However no power, human nor natural, could separate Njegoš from Montenegro. And today he still lives on in his people, and his words are remembered and passed on to today's Montenegrins. They are a lasting measure of wisdom and moral rightness.

182.
A "katun"
on Mt.
Lovćen with
Njegoš's
Mausoleum
in the
background

Prince Danilo

Njegoš was succeeded by Danilo Petrović, who was proclaimed prince. His leadership was energetic and hard. As a result of this internal opposition was fomented with which he dealt in a merciless and rude way.

He spent almost the whole of his 8 years of rule in conflict with the Turks. In the changed European circumstances his successes reverberated widely, but still not enough to gain formal recognition for Montenegro amongst the most powerful countries in the world. Danilo developed wide reaching diplomatic activities, and finally succeeded, with the guarantees of Russia and France, in coming to an agreement on borders with the Turks. This de facto meant international recognition of his state, even though this formally took another 20 years.

In foreign affairs, alongside the traditional dependence on Russia, he grew close to France. By doing so he strengthened the already powerful opposition which had been created by his own temperamental character, the brutality with which he dealt with rebellious tribes and his self will in leadership. Prince Danilo criticized and insulted many people. He was killed in revenge in Kotor in 1860 by the bullets of one of the humiliated Montenegrins.

King Nikola

The last ruler in the Petrović - Njegoš dynasty was Prince, later King, Nikola. He ruled Montenegro for over half a century. Actually it is more accurate to say that Montenegro ruled him. In the wars of this tortured and poverty-stricken country, with a powerful traditional tribal influence, with neck breaking roads, and without schools or culture, this wasn't the place for any sort of rulership.

When he wasn't leading the army in battle he dedicated himself to the spiritual renewal of his nation. He opened schools, grammar schools, and sowed the seeds of the idea of a university. He built a theatre, founded the National Library, State Museum and Archives. He resurrected the printing press, and started several magazines and newspapers. He liberally used the help of famous people from the worlds of culture, art and science, who were frequent and welcome guests at the palace. Thanks to his own education, but also to people whose ideas he respected, he was happy to quickly apply the latest technical achievements. Thus Montenegro was better connected internally but also was brought closer to the outside world. Prince Nikola stimulated development of trade and craftsmanship, but above all else agriculture. Every single soldier had to plant at least one olive tree. Tax exemptions helped those who worked and those

183.
Prince Danilo (author: Johann Bess, 1853); collections of State Museum in Cetinje

who owned. In other words he brought in a whole new epoch in the economic and cultural renewal of Montenegro.

During his long reign he literally lived with his subjects, adapting to their faults and strengths. In this way he sought to win them over to his ambitious state-education project.

He was very careful in the way he related to the people's national and religous feelings. He was deeply and personally part of the Serbian Orthodox Church and showed this by building and restoring monasteries and churches. But he ensured that Roman Catholics and Muslims had equal religous and other rights. He gave them, as full citizens of his princedom, full access to state services. This concern paid him back abundantly.

Prince Nikola led Montenegro in five wars. Right at the beginning and again right at the end of his rule the luck of war turned its back on him. In the other three wars Montenegro and the Montenegrins emerged with wreaths of glory, and he showed personal bravery and exceptional war skills. He made war wisely and with a clear state programme, which is evidence that he preeminently sought prosperity for his nation in the politics of lasting peace, work, national well-being and advancement. The war aims of Montenegro never deviated from that of a justified struggle for the liberation and unifying of the Yugoslav nations, and above all else the unification of the Serbian peoples.

During the whole course of his reign Nikola developed excellent diplomatic ties. Many would agree to the claim that he was the best diplomat among the Yugoslav nations in the Balkans. Grasping the reality of the world in which he lived, he knew the power and importance of decisions made around the "green table". He didn't hold back from talking to, visiting, even pleading with the great powers in order to strengthen and ensure the international acceptance of Montenegro.

He ran his own family with this aim in mind. By marrying five of his daughters off to powerful European palaces

184. King Nikola (author: Paja Jovanović, 1903); collections of State Museum in Cetinje

(they called him "Europe's Father-in-law") he had direct access and significant influence on the European and world centres of power. Cetinje was at that time one of the diplomatic centres of the Balkans, and the name of Montenegro was uttered with a kind of mystic respect in Europe.

Finally as a result of war victories over the Turks, and the diplomatic skill of Prince Nikola, Montenegro was recognised as a free and independent state at the Berlin Congress of 1878.

Nikola Petrović in foreign affairs relied mainly on the support of Russia, but succeeded in keeping good relations with other countries, especially with Montenegro's great and powerful neighbours, Turkey, Italy and Austria. Against some of them he could wage merciless war, and then cooperate in times of peace.

Probably it was foreign affairs that led him on the fiftieth anniversary of his reign to proclaim Montenegro a kingdom, and himself king. Although the results of his rulership were impressive in every respect this was now the waning of his political star.

Internal opposition within Montenegro, a result of the conflict between the liberal democratic tendencies of young intellectuals and the despotic form of rule, as well as the dramatic events occurring at the time (the two Balkan wars and the First World War), led to capitulation to the Austro-Hungarian forces and Nikola's leaving Montenegro in 1916.

The Montenegrin army found itself without a commander and without a state, but didn't give in. They halted the many times greater enemy at the famous Battle of Mojkovac and thus enabled the Serbian army to escape from their country, occupied by the Austro-Hungarians but not defeated. After capitulation the Montenegrin army converted into an armed nation and continued the struggle.

At the Versailles Peace Conference after the First World War, among the victors' tables was one with the title Montenegro. No one sat there but it had to be present. The reason for this was the attitude of the Great Powers. At the end of 1918 in Podgorica the Great National Assembly voted for union with Serbia and the other Yugoslav nations.

The Petrović - Njegoš dynasty was dethroned, and King Nikola was forbidden to return to Montenegro.

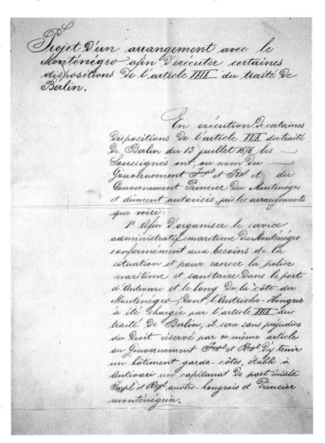

185.
The Treaty of Berlin of 1878 by which Montenegro became an internationally recognized state; collections of State Museum in Cetinje

186.
A King Nikola's handgun (19th c.); collections of State Museum in Cetinje

THE MODERN TRADITIONALISM OF THE MONTENEGRINS

The inclusion of Montenegro in Yugoslavia represented the realisation of the centuries old desire of the best minds of all Yugoslav nationalities. In many respects similar these nations had been constantly divided amongst the powerful states which controlled the Balkans. Dreaming of freedom they had a vision of their own united brotherly state.

But you can place the whole world between dreams and reality. Montenegro lost its for centuries defended statehood and in return received little or nothing. The period between the two world wars didn't produce the desired progress either materially nor spiritually. Montenegro was left as an unnamed internal province of Yugoslavia, under the Karadjordjević dynasty.

The beginning of the Second World War saw the defeat of Yugoslavia and capitulation to the fascist coalition. Montenegro was occupied by Italy. In the beginning this was a "soft" occupation. The Italians counted on the friendly feelings which Montenegrins fostered towards the Italians, especially from the time when Jelena daughter of King Nikola became the Italian Queen. A quisling regime was even formed which congratulated Montenegrins for their "freedom" under the Italian army.

Then a miracle once again occurred.

The answer to this dishonourable offer arrived the next day. The whole of Montenegro rose in revolt.

This was the first mass, all-encompassing resistance to fascism in the whole of enslaved Europe. Again the world wondered at the courage and endurance of the Montenegrin people. New divisions arrived in Montenegro and the occupier shot 10 hostages, innocent civilians, for every one lost soldier.

The war lasted a full 4 years. Montenegrin partisan units fought as part of the national liberation army, which grew to the fourth largest force in the anti-fascist coalition. One of the most significant results of that struggle was that Montenegro decided to be an equal federal unit in the new, second Yugoslavia. Because of the undeniable role of the Communist Party during the war, the patriotism and bravery of its members, its role in political life was inviolable.

Within the Socialist Federal Republic of Yugoslavia Montenegro entered a half century period of peace, the longest such period in its turbulent history. The Socialist system was not as rigid as in some other countries. Due to this there were huge advances materially and spiritually. Montenegro completely changed its character. By all important criteria Montenegro is among the ranks of the medium developed countries of the world. In areas where special attention was paid results were even better. Montenegro as a whole and especially the coast became a famous European tourist destination.

187.
Citadel in the Old Town of Budva

In the area of material and spiritual development almost all the dreams of the founders of the Montenegrin state and its tradition of freedom were finally realised. Illiteracy was almost completely irradicated. The average educational attainments of the population were exceptionally high in comparison with other countries at the same level of development. The entire population was covered by social security. Montenegro was linked with the world by relatively modern communications.

However new times brought expectations and needs which were an inescapable part of modern everyday life. But in the gap between these and the method of satisfying them the socialist system, personified in the ruling Communist Party, lost the battle. The democratic changes which the former socialist countries experienced at the start of the nineties changed the political world map. The process and the effects of such large and rapid changes in individual countries were dramatic, but the whole process will certainly be judged by history as good for the civilised population.

There was a premonition of these events in Montenegro. That is almost a year before the Berlin Wall fell there was a quiet and soft revolution, which uprooted half a century of political life and the values created by this. Work on democratizing the state, developing parliamentarism, and a multi-party system began alongside a strengthening of the free market, the widening of human rights and the protection of man's basic freedoms. Actually it was more a case of evolution, seeing as dramatic events normally associated with revolutionary takeovers were completely avoided.

Of course none of this was very interesting to a world with too much of its own problems to give attention to a small country peacefully and patiently trying to find its place in the given circumstances. But this is a fate to which Montenegro has long been accustomed.

However to those who were absorbed in the above described events one thing drew particular attention. This could be termed the modern traditionalism of the Montenegrins.

On numerous occasions throughout the centuries this nation has shown its amazing ability to overcome easily the difficult and even the impossible. On the other hand that which was easy and straightforward for others to achieve, took many years in Montenegro. There are examples of this at every step.

The real cause of this cannot be found without an overall look at history and the circumstances under which Montenegro existed and which changed the national consciousness, rules and traditions.

Montenegrins are constantly looking deep into their glorious past. In the face of these great examples the fear that one will not live up to one's forbears is very understandable. In the desire to leave after oneself as many good works as possible lies the strength for great challenges and zeal. Thus the past and future are united in the present. Glances directed at the past reveal future paths.

Surrounded by difficult circumstances, living from day to day, they were freed of many worldly concerns which are nice for the body but can soften up the spirit. Thus an integral part of their greatness is the normal human weaknesses which give them a specific charm and individuality. Great works here can suffer from small temptations, and normal human weakness sometimes hides general human values.

On the other hand one of the basic characteristics of the struggle for self-preservation is the ability to adapt, openness to innovation. Inspite of strong traditionalism, Montenegro was and remains open to new social relations and social achievements.

In Montenegro women very early received political rights, including the right to vote. Radio-telegraph and car traffic, as revolutionary technical achievements of their age soon found a place in this small state which in reality at the time had other needs to concentrate on rather than following the developed world in technical innovation. Montenegrins on numerous occasions surprised Europe with their ability to adapt to unknown circumstances. Those who grew up in Montenegro or bore its genes, very quickly learnt the rules of life in other surroundings. Today throughout the globe as respected and recognised citizens of their new homelands, they keep their love for their "old home" and make their Montenegro even more proud and beautiful.

In Montenegro itself many generations of young people have come of age who are in every respect the same as their equivalents from big and developed countries. They play and speak and work as citizens of the world in the 21st century. At the same time they all carry a deep consciousness of their uniqueness and proudly proclaim their allegiance to Montenegro.

Modern traditionalism thus lives on.

By character and temperament Montenegrins, like the majority of highlanders, are hospitable and kind towards strangers and have friendly feelings towards those who agree with their high ideals about independence and devotion to one's country.

Sir John Gardner Wilkinson (1797 - 1875)
British archaeologist

188.
The village of Javorje on Mt. Durmitor

n modern times the sense of fulfillment to be received by discovering new, unknown regions and unusual human communities has been greatly decreased. The global linking of civilisation has imposed its own rules. Many airports, hotels, even entire cities around the world look just like each other. The modern way of life has linked almost the whole population of the planet and has enforced certain rules of behaviour and has decreased the distance which separates people. Standards and procedures of human behaviour have become a necessary condition of the survival of our civilisation.

However even in these circumstances each people and each state has many individual characteristics which makes them distinguishable. Man's connection with nature is unbreakable so that people starting with physical characteristics and going on to the way of life, carry the stamp of the environment where they were born. And historical events, that is to say the collective consciousness and experiences which arise out of them, also create characteristics which differentiate parts of the one planet and the same human race.

Many people around the world have written about the Montenegrins and their small but excitingly beautiful country. Over 100,000 bibliographic articles and references by foreigners to Montenegro have been systematized and scientifically examined. The life and customs of Montenegrins have been a rich inspiration to many intelligent people, and their judgment has been given special attention in Montenegro. One of the constant desires of Montenegrins is to be respected and affirmed, based on the maxim that it isn't so important what one thinks of oneself but rather what others think of you.

191

189-190.
The Dobri Do "katun" (at 1,457 m) on Mt. Durmitor
191.
Tepca in Durmitor National Park

192.
Pirni Do on Mt. Durmitor
193.
Apron - hand-made
by women from Vasojevići
(a region in the north-east of Montenegro)

193

WARRIORS WITH GENEROUS SPIRITS

The Montenegrin way of life for centuries was dictated by wars, that is to say the unmerciful struggle for survival in freedom. The "constant struggle", lasting more than half a millennium, of a small nation which decided to oppose the plans of the then great powers and mighty empires. The freedom which that struggle won became the most precious value in Montenegro, and those who proved themselves most in the numerous battles represent the best examples to those around them. A people especially cultured and civilised for the Middle Ages paid a high price for their own independence and freedom. Withdrawing into the barely passable mountains and defending with almost impossible endurance their ravines and passes, they defeated many times more powerful armies. However they also experienced a fall in their level of civilisation, as the inevitable result of isolation, war and life in inhospitable climes.

Even at the beginning of the 19th century European chroniclers wrote: "Montenegro is the only European country where there is not one single town, not even a village that you could compare with a town." The explanation for this strange fact comes from the same pen: "Always open to the danger of the Turk enslaving them, the Montenegrins have no other interest but to defend themselves from that barbaric neighbour. Art, science, literature, those ideals of European glory, mean nothing to them. The Montenegrin is happy with a gun, a sword and a Bible, which he kisses more than reads. Because of this he is maybe happier in so far as it is true that man is happiest when he is near to nature".

The conditions of life influenced the development of the special physical and psychological characteristics of this nation. Physical ability had to be particularly stressed because of the difficult conditions of survival and the effect of natural selection. This contributed to the normal temperance in matters of food and drink, the avoiding of harmful habits, a simple way of life, and a healthy living environment. Many travel writers were amazed at the physical appearance of the then Montenegrin men and women and thoroughly described their physical particularities. And even today there are strong evidences of this inheritance. Modern science says that Montenegrins are marked by strong constitutions and above average growth, such that together with some African tribes they can be considered as true giants. According to statistics from draft commissions Montenegrins are on average the tallest in Europe.

Alongside this Montenegrins have created a special spiritual climate. Their habits, customs, value system and moral principles form a unique life philosophy. The influences which bore on them have left a very strong mark right up to the present day. In the central and northern parts of Montenegro there are clear signs of the Ottoman culture in language, habits dress... The

Montenegro has developed heroism to a level comparable to Thermopylae and Marathon, if not more, considering the far fewer numerical and material resources at their disposal, and the fact that their opponent is by far braver and stronger.
William Ewart Gladstone (1809 - 1898), English statesman

194. *Vlaška Church in Cetinje, with the fence made of rifle barrels captured in battles*

south-eastern parts shared culture and customs with Albanian tribes; and on the coast living communication with Italy, and through it with developed Europe, is clearly evident. However all these additions have passed through a thick net of local moral values and were selectively and critically accepted.

The life of Montenegrins had to be strictly organised and laid out, without any ambiguity as to aims and values. Family, brotherhood, tribe and the whole state upheld the military spirit of the time. A strict hierarchy of authority existed - father, elders, tribal chief, ruler. From this a strong sense of collectivism, patriarchalism and traditionalism are deep in the consciousness of every Montenegrin. It's like when people in the mountains are overtaken by a blizzard and hide in some cave staying close to each other so as not to lose their body heat.

Love for freedom isn't obviously only the preserve of Montenegrins. But amongst Montenegrins this feeling has reached the level of an obsession, (they have become "slaves to their freedom") seeing how there are few nations who would be so willing to pay such a high price for freedom and independence, a price which appears irrational or perhaps impossible to some. So dedicated to the cult of freedom are the Montenegrins that they made decisions which decided not only their own fate but that of future generations.

For long in Montenegro there was only one certainty, that there would be wars and battles in which it was necessary to show your heroism and thus pay your debt to your homeland. When a male child was born, alongside special ceremonies and celebrations that the country had received one more defender, a gun was placed on the cradle to get the baby used to what he would be doing throughout his life. In those times literally everyone was a soldier. Even men 100 years old considered it their duty to stand and defend their homeland and to seek death on the field of battle. Many women also fought with gun in hand, whilst the others brought up the rear, helping their fathers, husbands, and sons. Military analysts of the time stated that, ".. in the event of an unexpected attack, you can count on with absolute certainty, that at the first alert as many soldiers will set off for the area under attack as there are men in the country. Of course not all are ready to fight, but all are willing to help." The modern approach to war, practiced in this century with tragic results in the First and Second World Wars, has not changed the desire and ability of the Montenegrin people to rise up and defend their freedom and independence.

*195.
A "gusle" (one-string fiddle) player from Durmitor*

Montenegro nowadays still keeps alive in memory a long line of its decorated, heroes in the struggle for freedom. There is no monument to the unknown soldier here, since they made their name and received glory on the field of battle and have been remembered and their tales passed on from knee to knee.

However heroism alone as a high moral value was never enough for one to enter into the national memory. For someone to be remembered for all time their heroism had to be accompanied with a higher moral value known as "Čojstvo" - manhood. "Čojstvo" is the term for a collection of the highest moral strengths. In the national understanding heroism is to defend yourself from someone else, čojstvo is defending others from yourself. When the nation wants to give someone its highest compliment it simply calls the person "Čovjek", a Man, and this adjectival noun has gained its own life philosophy and historical inheritance.

The chivalrous relationship to other people, even to the most mortal enemy, is a clear evidence that the Montenegrins - these passionate warriors and brave defenders, are in essence generous people who never wanted to, nor knew how to, hate others. They only loved their freedom and didn't see defending it as a sin that anyone should punish them for.

The Montenegrin was always a warrior but never a cold calculating man who looks upon war as some kind of interest. His wars were ones of virtue and faith that every nation and every man has the right to freedom and a decent life. Force against force, and for everything else warm human words - was recommended by the national leaders, and the nation didn't ignore this, but rather added yet more examples of heroism and manhood. Thus there has been constant repeated evidence that the Montenegrin Man is made up of all the virtues in which he believes and which he seeks after.

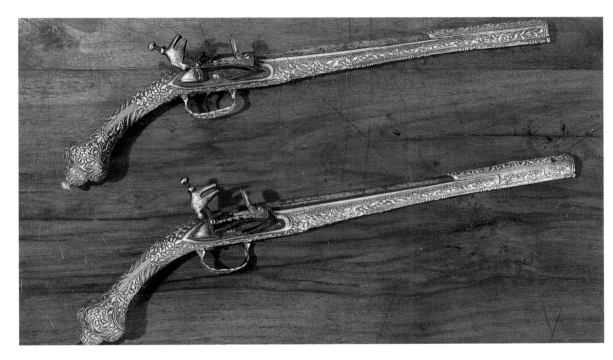

196.
Gold-plated silver pistols made and decorated in Kotor (13th c.); collections of Maritime Museum in Kotor

The Montenegrin was therefore by force of circumstances a warrior. He became a generous person by his own choice. In this symbiosis the human and the warrior were not in tension. The warrior in him defended his rights without withdrawal, and humanity caused him to respect the personality and rights of others as if his own. This is evidenced by the numerous acts of chivalry, generousity and respect towards enemies.

The words of the Montenegrin hero Novica Cerović who killed the great enemy and Turkish hero Smail-aga Čengić have remained, "I'm a man and I won't withdraw from human nature. What is life? A struggle. When God gave me life He made me a fighter, and I am always ready to fight heroically amongst the ranks of my own. Whatever is human, within that is wrong, deceit and prejudice. The short sighted man cannot clearly see the difference between right and wrong. Whether it is one or the other, whatever my nation fights for, that

*197.
Medun near
Podgorica, the
birthplace of
Marko
Miljanov*

*198.
Marko
Miljanov (19th
c.). A re-
nowned hero
and "vojvoda"
(duke)*

198

for me is the highest law. I respect every enemy only when I know he keeps his word, is hospitable, and that he honourably engages in wrestling hand to hand. Whoever is overcome, killed, is no longer an enemy. Beyond the grave is another life of which I have no idea."

At the end of the Great War against the Turks (1878), after the absolute victory of Montenegrin arms, deep inside Montenegrin territory was stranded the surrounded Turkish garrison of Medun. There was no hope of help from anywhere. The Turkish commander offered surrender to Duke Marko Miljanov, hero and thinker who described the difference between heroism and manhood. He said that they were forced to surrender because they no longer had water, food or munitions. Duke Marko didn't accept the surrender of opponents in trouble so he ordered that the Turks be given all that they lacked. After three days of fighting the Montenegrins overcame the fortress. There was great rejoicing amongst the people and the army. But the Duke ordered that rejoicing ceased until the last prisoner had left the hill on the road to Cetinje. He explained, "We mustn't humiliate an honourable and brave enemy."

Towards the beginning of the Second World War an Italian division was fighting the partisan brigade "Marko Miljanov". The Italians were heavily defeated. About one hundred wounded soldiers were left on the field of battle. Because some of them would have to spend the night under open skies the Montenegrin partisans put beside each wounded Italian soldier a glass of water, a glass of honey and a lit candle, so that their own side would find them more easily. The chivalrous gesture of Marko Miljanov wasn't an exception but more of a moral example to warriors with generous spirits.

Many ideals of a modern citizen state of which with justification old Europe and the new world are proud, were born in Montenegro in the intoxication of freedom and an unstinting struggle for freedom. And although for Montenegro and its people almost the highest joy was in protecting independence, the fact that a hero and warrior must be a man was never forgotten, and that means one who never gives way to the inhuman. One who knows how to fight but also to live in peace and to forgive. Thus struggling against many powerful enemies and conquerors, Montenegrins also fought with themselves.

Happy is the nation who wins these sort of battles.

FAITH IN PEOPLE AND GOD

During their turbulent history the Montenegrins have developed a special relationship with God. The Orthodox christian faith has a powerful element of togetherness, that is to say affirmation of the national will. There is no rigid church hierarchy, there are many churches, but as a rule they are small, and the priests live the life of their believers. These general characteristics of Orthodoxy are even more pronounced in Montenegro. As a free territory surrounded by the Ottoman Empire, for a long time the development of natural relationships with the rest of the orthodox world and in general Christendom were impossible. Thus the national characteristics of the Church were strengthened. Alongside this the priesthood wasn't particularly well educated in the faith, but they excelled amongst the people, including involvement in the armed struggle against the conquerors.

Starting from the fact that God made man in his own image, Montenegrins tried to reach God in man and to find man in God. They sought God in their own image. Thus one of the clear thinking Montenegrin Bishops in his time noted that Montenegrins in their relationship with God were on first name terms. In fact it is very easy to see that the highest moral values amongst Montenegrins completely correspond to the basic ethical postulates of Orthodox Christianity. Faith was and remains a basic component of life, built into everyday customs, more from a strict respect of the virtues and protection from sin than from fear of the coming "judgment day".

This is why it is possible here to find deep and sincere believers who don't know the basic prayers, or who have rarely entered a church.

Loyalty to its faith is one of the century old foundations of the survival of Montenegro and its people. They entered into the struggle for freedom alongside the cross, the symbol of faith and the eternal virtues which override the meaning of the life of any individual. For what else is faith but the connection between the limited human and the unlimited Divine? The connection which represents the hope that, with the help of the one who created heaven and earth, human temptation and weakness can be overcome.

With the help of such a faith - which doesn't close the door to civilisation's achievements and which encompasses within itself understanding, common sense and courage - the Montenegrin rulers and people sincerely sought God's mercy in helping them to judge reasonably and to distinguish good from evil.

The ability to in everything, and above all in every man, to look for and find a higher purpose, in Montenegro led to an exceptionally high tolerance between religions. That which is now a precondition of the survival of civilisation on this planet and its democratic development, has for centuries been practiced here. Despite temporary and heavy conflict between nations divided by various religions, the obligation to respect other religions and to protect their symbols is enthroned here. Thanks to this culture various religous communities dwell here in ecumenical understanding, many new churches and places of worship oriented to understanding and good people are being built and old ones restored.

In Montenegro there are 955 religious buildings. Of these 650 are Orthodox churches and monasteries, 177 are Roman Catholic and 128 Muslim mosques. There are many past and present examples of how neighbours divided by faith but joined by a common destiny and everyday life, cooperate and help each other irrespective of the current relationships between the leaders of their religions or their ethnic homelands. This turbulent history has become a harmonious present where differences between people and their beliefs aren't wrong but actually bring richness to a society.

Faith in people and in God with a human face is sowed into people from an early age within their families. The family has weathered all the storms of temptation, including the most modern and strongest which is brought by today's way of life. And today in the modern Montenegrin family the powerful connection between its members and their readiness to help each other cross all life's temptations together is very clearly marked.

The way of life involving collectivism and patriachalism which was necessary for survival has long been superseded. But even the most modern man has a need to be linked with people with whom he is connected by birth, spiritual closeness, even fate. Thus family customs have not only survived difficult times, but are stronger having taken a new form adapted to the demands of modern times. Man's happiness is increased when it is shared with his nearest and dearest, and his sorrow lessened by the sincere sympathy and help of his own and numerous other families.

Special emphasis is given to the family saint's day, the "slava", in Montenegrin households. This is a religous ritual in praise of a church saint who has been chosen as the family protector. In honour of the "household god" the entire family gets together. The most beautiful and best table available is brought into the dining area for that special day. Dear friends are welcomed into the house, and the whole ritual has far more human warmth than religous ceremony.

In the family stories from the glorious past are passed on to the young generation and the basic ethical values are emphasized. Grandfathers talk about how it was in the long distant and magnificent days, and the wide-eyed grand-children drink in the pictures glorifying heroism, manhood, respect, love of truth, hospitality... Acts which were contrary to these are remembered, passed on and judged. Often these lessons are learnt before primary school days, but as a rule are remembered for a lifetime.

Thus the "word" has taken on almost a magical significance. Thus the beautiful word which is passed on and extols what has been done becomes a link with eternity. It is worth dying for this word for without it life has little meaning. One's word had to be measured and kept to. The word unsheathed and sheathed the sword and carried the fate of many human beings. Consideration in the use of the word bore wisdom, as an exceptionally valuable virtue. Those who used the ability of the human spirit to find the best means to achieve goals are considered wise people. The national language today is full of sayings which with the wisdom of Socrates, point in the direction of the dilemmas of life.

The role of women in every and especially in the Montenegrin family is exceptionally significant. Today women have conquered wide areas of equality with men - the heads of the

199.
The bells
of the Ostrog
Monastery

family. Girl students in Montenegro are in the majority, women are educated and carry out complex and important jobs. However their role in the history of Montenegro has been insufficiently recognised. They weren't predestined for achievement. Their heroism was all the same exceptional because it was daily. They were the cornerstone and foundation on which each family rested. Modest but decisive they didn't categorize jobs into male and female. While their husbands were constantly at war they provided materially for the survival of their families and the state. Alongside this they were an ever flowing spring of love which they sowed in their children, rejoicing each day they were together, before they would be separated by the brutal circumstances that almost every generation was brought up in.

From this grew up the cult of mother, sister, women in general as an oasis of peace, love and warmth which lives on now in Montenegro. Motives of self-preservation and safeguarding the family name meant that Montenegrins were more joyful with male children. But as a rule they loved more, or at least showed more gentleness towards, their female descendants. Proud and brave heroes who were unafraid in the face of any danger to protect their country and beliefs, were and remain powerless before the beautiful life of a child, that most important member of humanity.

The Montenegrin way of life and their sincere love for people developed also hospitality as a valued ethical norm. Right up to very recently, until the development of road communications and the hotel and inn trade, it was considered a requirement to put up and feed travellers who would knock on the door. The warmth of the hearth was shared with them and if necessary the last piece of bread. This custom, of course, has been significantly changed in recent times, but it hasn't been completely lost. It is especially seen in the development of tourism. One of the important advantages that Montenegro offers tourists is the hospitality that flows from direct contact with people and which goes beyond the necessary courtesy for this economic activity.

In the tragic events arising from the recent civil war in the area of previous Yugoslavia, the citizens of Montenegro have shown exceptional hospitality. Montenegro has accepted refugees which represent 12 percent of its total population. Statisticians say that this has broken the world record for caring for people brought to a new region because of war and disaster. It should be especially emphasized that these people are not being put up in any kind of collective camps or accommodation, but have rather found a place to stay in the modest homes of normal Montenegrins.

Every disaster passes but human acts remain and are remembered, would say the old and wise Montenegrins. Good must be returned with good.

Sometimes abandoned and forgotten by all but God, Montenegro has gained in experience by remembering virtues and protecting the good right at that dramatic crossing of the eternal and the temporal.

Belief in man and God was and remains stronger than any disbelief and doubt.

200.
Crvena Greda on Mt. Durmitor

All traces of the previous
population and their state
organisation have disappeared from
the consciousness of the nation
and there are no written documents.
Archaeological remains, which
because of the general conditions
existing throughout the ages have
never been properly examined,
give only a faint hint
of the far past.

201.
A Hellenistic cup (4th-1st c.); Budva

CULTURAL HERITAGE AND THE ARTS

*M*ontenegro has preserved the integral nature of its cultural and spiritual wealth through all the periods of its development and despite the numerous changes of its name and borders. Therefore, Montenegro has inherited everything that has been created in its present day territory and keeps it in its too rich treasury.

THE VESTIGES OF BYGONE DAYS

Although prehistory remains ultimately unfathomable, there is ample evidence that the territory of Montenegro has been inhabited by man since time immemorial. Indeed, it is one of the largest Stone Age sites in Europe.

Crvena Stijena, near Podgorica, is the oldest prehistoric archaeological site in Montenegro. Its archaeological cross-section has been found to consist of thirty-one layers, and experts have not yet unearthed them all.

About 3,000 years ago prehistoric people painted images of amazing beauty on the walls of a cave at the village of Lipci, near Risan. The most remarkable of these paintings are a deer hunting scene and a realistic depiction of a boat, the only such representation in Montenegro's prehistoric art.

These ancient boats have not changed to this day. After more than two thousand years, they still sail upon Lake Skadar. Light and swift, with long and narrow hulls, pointed bows and shallow draughts, these vessels are regarded as the most elegant craft in the Mediterranean.

202.
Cave drawings
from the Bronze
age; Risan

The copper cruciform axe, dating from about 2,000 B.C. and discovered at Tuzi, near Podgorica, belongs to the culture of an Illyrian tribe called the Labeats.

But it is Montenegro's ancient coastal towns that encompass all historical periods. Ulcinj, Bar, Budva, Kotor and Risan are exquisite illustrations of ancient architectural mastery. The centres of these cities are impressive examples of cultural development carried across the warm seas. In antiquity, living at sea meant being at the centre of the world.

Budva is the oldest town on the Montenegrin coast. Originally an Illyrian settlement, its age is estimated at 2,500 years. A Greek market, emperion, was built later. The first written reference to Budva was made by the famous Greek tragedian, Sophocles, in the 5th century B.C. The town also boasts the largest and most magnificent necropolis on the Adriatic coast. The Illyrian, Hellenistic, Roman, late-antique and early Slavic archaeological layers reveal the life, culture and customs of the people who lived in this region in different periods of history. Most of the valuable objects, notably golden jewellery from the 3rd century B.C., date from the Hellenistic period.

Risan is another important ancient settlement. There are no valuable artefacts from its earliest period, when it was the capital of the Illyrian queen Teuta. The first truly magnificent archaeological finds date from the 2nd century, when the area was ruled by Rome. Standing out among the splendid Roman polychrome floor mosaics is a representation of Hypnos, the Greek god of sleep, the only depiction of this deity in the Balkans. Other beautiful finds from the Risan necropolis include the torso and head of the Roman emperor Domitian.

Ulcinj's sacrificial altar from the 5th century B.C., dedicated by Greek stone cutters to Artemis, the goddess of deer hunting, is one of the most important works of art from the time this ancient town came under Hellenic influence. The inscription on the altar is the oldest one on the eastern Adriatic coast.

Doclea was the largest and most important town on the territory of present-day Montenegro in Roman times. Named after the Docleats, an Illyrian tribe that inhabited the Zeta basin, it was probably founded in the 1st century. Though protected by three rivers and a moat, it was not spared destruction. It was never rebuilt after the Avar and Slavic onslaughts in the early 6th century. It is an archaeological site of world renown, explored by Europe's most famous archaeologists. Necropoles dating back to the period from the 1st to the 4th century have been excavated here. As a completely urbanized settlement, it has left many vestiges of Roman culture, especially stone sculpture with valuable inscriptions.

UNESCO has declared Kotor part of the world's natural and cultural heritage. The town is remarkable for the architectural style of its buildings and its 4.5 km-long ramparts. The construction of these fortifications began in Illyrian times and lasted up until the 18th century. The Slavicization of Kotor's Roman population began in the 7th century, and by the 11th century the name of the town had assumed its Slavic form. The town's imposing 12th-century Cathedral of St Triphon is most representative of the Romanesque architecture on the Adriatic coast. The Byzantine emperor Constantine VII Porphyrogenetus ("crimson-born"), who lived in the 10th century, made a reference to a 9th-century church on whose ruins the Cathedral of St Triphon was later erected.

203. Budva

Second only to this cathedral in historical significance is the building of the Kotor Navy, a brotherhood of seamen established in the 9th century. The first written reference to it is from the 12th century. It is one of the oldest naval organizations in the world, whose statutes were laid down in the 15th century. A professional, military, humanitarian and cultural association, it has been very successful in keeping its glorious past from falling into oblivion. Kotor's Church of St Luke was also built in the 12th century in Byzantine-Romanesque style and has been preserved in its original form.

Other gems of Montenegro's cultural heritage include the Bar Archbishopric, the Zeta Bishopric, the Benedictine Monasteries of Our Lady on Cape Ratec, the remains of Prečista Krajinska Monastery, which in the 15th century was the seat of the Zeta Metropolitan, and the Church of St Peter in Bijelo Polje.

CHURCH BOOKS AND FRESCOES

For centuries Montenegrin churches have been more than just places of worship. They have served as schools, sanctuaries for the persecuted and even forts from which attacks were successfully repelled. For a long time they were the only centres of social life, fulfilling the function of the forum in ancient Greece or of various cultural institutions of today.

The Chronicle of the Doclean Priest and Miroslav's Gospel, two documents of unparalleled cultural value, originated in the 12th century.

The Chronicle, also known as The Empire of the Slavs, is the only domestic source of historical data from the period preceding the 12th century. This historico-literary work was written by an unknown author in the Bar area in the second half of the 12th century. It was the first work of its kind among the South Slavs. Its twenty-three chapters, originally written in a Slavic language, have been preserved only in their Latin translations. Full of references to Doclea, Serbia, Croatia and Macedonia, The Chronicle is a highly important source of information for those studying the history of the Balkan Slavs. Its second half begins with a legendary tale of the Zeta prince Vladimir. It is a wonderfully poetical love novel, with subtle psychological nuances, on a par with the much better known works of its kind written in Europe several centuries later.

204

The cult of St Vladimir is associated with the Cross of St Vladimir, which has for centuries been treasured by a family from the Bar area. Once a year the cross is brought to the top of Mt Rumija. Orthodox Christians, Catholics and Muslims all take part in the ritual, believing that this is the very cross referred to in the legend of Prince Vladimir.

205

204.
Roman mosaics (3rd c.); Risan
205.
Emperor Domitian (1st c.); collections of Maritime Museum in Kotor
206.
Remains of the Roman city of Doclea (Duklja, 1st to 6th c.)

Montenegro undoubtedly takes one of the first places;
the legendary heroism of her people brings honour to mankind.
Giuseppe Garibaldi (1807 - 1882), Italian politician

207.
Old Kotor surrounded by 4.5 km long walls
208.
View of Kotor
209.
National costumes of Boka and Montenegro

Miroslav's Gospel is the oldest known document written in standard language and the oldest illuminated manuscript in medieval Zeta. Copied in the 1180s and adorned with nearly three hundred initials and miniatures, it is an exquisite combination of the Byzantine and Romanesque styles. The initials represent stylised animals and plants, real and fantastic, joined to human figures. The miniatures contain Mediterranean, Byzantine-Romanesque and early-Serbian ornaments. Written by two different authors, it also incorporates two different variants of the Old Slavonic language - those used in the Zeta-Hum and Ras areas. The ornaments in this book bring East and West together through their visual resplendence and creative unity.

Morača monastery and its single-naved church, were built in the canyon of the Morača river in the mid-13th century. For over seventy years in the 16th century the interior of the church was exposed to the skies, as its lead roof had been taken away by the Turks. Only fragments of paintings from the diaconicon have been preserved from that period, but they still constitute the height of Byzantine fresco-painting among the South Slavs. The monastery was the centre of Zeta's wall painting in the 13th century. The style of this school was more flexible than that of the Byzantine school of fresco painting. The frescoes in Morača monastery have bright and unobtrusive colours, and their delicate lines and the beauty of the faces, postures and movements bear comparison with the works of ancient masters.

The Gorica Compendium, composed in 1441-1442, is associated with Jelena Balšić, daughter of the Serbian prince Lazar. It contains, among other things, the correspondence between Jelena and her confessor, Nicon of Jerusalem. At Jelena's request, Andrija Izat, Kotor's most famous goldsmith of the 14th and 15th centuries, made a silver frame for The Compendium and adorned its front cover with a figure of Christ.

There was a notary's office in Kotor as early as the 12th century, but no notarial records before 1326 have survived. The 300 remaining notarial books are the most reliable written documents about life in Boka and old Montenegro over several historical periods.

The Octoechos (a hymn book) is the first book among the South Slavs printed in Cyrillic script. The last copies of it came out of the printing office founded by Zeta's last medieval ruler, Djurdje Crnojević, on 4 January 1494. Typeset by the hieromonk Macarius, it had 597 pages in two different colours and was adorned with Renaissance initials and figural compositions.

The Crnojević press was founded only forty years after the publication of the first printed book, Gutenberg's Bible (1445). For a long time the books printed by the Crnojević press set standards for presses founded outside present-day Montenegro.

366

multum temporis in bello mortuus est in Chelmani[a].

XLIV. Interea populi, congregantes se, constituerunt regem *V*ladimirum, filium Vladimiri, filii regis Michala. Regnante illo, dilexit pacem et cum omnibus pacem habuit. Congregavitque ad se omnes fratres suos et accepit uxorem filiam iupani Rassae; et quievit terra XII annos. Postquam accepit rex filiam Belcani, dimissus est a iupano rex Dobroslavus, qui tenebatur in vinculis, eo quod esset patruus regis Vladimiri. Qui dimissus venit ad nepotem suum, quem ut vidit rex, statim comprehendere iussit et in custodiam ponere; mansitque in custodia usque quo nepos eius Vladimirus regnavit. Itaque XII^mo anno regni Vladimiri regis, Jaquinta, consiliata a quibusdam pessimis hominibus, qui inimici erant iupani Belcani, potionem mortiferam conficiens in Cattaro, quo manebat, dedit eis. Hii vero venientes in Scodarim propinaverunt regi per manus ministrorum eius, qui ab eis deceptus

esso Belcano cercare occasione co' suoi Rassiani di poter a qualche modo far morire Cocciaparo. Del che egli avvedutosi, si ritirò in Bosna, dove, tolta per moglie la figliuola del bano di Bosna, non molto dopo in un fatto d' arme fu ammazzato in Chelmo.

Ma i popoli dell' Illirico ch' erano assuefatti vivere sotto i re, crearono per loro re Vladimiro, nato da Vladimiro figliuolo di Michala, che (com' e stato detto) successe nel regno a Dobroslavo, primo di questo nome, suo padre. Costui per essere persona d'animo molto quieto, raccolse a se tutti quelli che erano del suo legnaggio verso a i quali mostrò grande amore. Et havendo tolto per moglie la figliuola di Belcano, conte di Rassia, la terra s' acchettò per ispatio di quindici anni. Et fu liberato da prigione re Dobroslavo da Belcano, il quale fece ciò per far cosa grata al suo genero Vladimiro. Questo Dobroslavo tosto che venne alla presenza di Vladimiro, fu per suo ordine incarcerato. Et cosi mentre egli regnò, vi stette. Il quinto decimo anno del regno di Vladimiro, Jaquinta moglie di Bodino già defunto, fatto il consiglio con alcuni huomini

*210.
"Ljetopis popa Dukljanina" (Doclean Priest's Chronicle 12th c.); collections of State Museum*

Ѫ КСЛІ · ИПОСЛȢШАЮС

ЖУ҇С · Д҇НЕ · Ѡ҇ЛЮ · ТА

Ѣ Ѡ · СЛЫШАКЬНРО

ЧЕ Т КОРОКЛАСТЬМ

ЪIКАЮЩАѠ НЕ ГО

НИ ЕДОМЕНШИКЫ

КАНЕ ГЛЕМОѤКЫ

Ѫ · ҇ ІКОНЕА N К

Ѡ МРЬТКЫ ХЪ

Ѣ ХЪЖЕ ІКОНАН

СЕ Ѡ ДРȢГНХЬ

211.
"Miroslavljevo jevandjelje" (Miroslav's Gospel), a manuscript: the oldest document written in a literary language; a photoset edition (1897); collections of State Museum
212.
"Raven feeding prophet Ilija (Elias)", a fresco in the Morača Monastery
213.
The Morača Monastery (built in 1252)
214-215.
The Morača Monastery: an icon and the door inlaid with ivory

241

These standards were also adhered to by the most prolific Montenegrin printer and publisher, Božidar Vuković Podgoričanin, who in the early 16th century founded a press for graphically ornamented Cyrillic books in Venice, Europe's major printing centre at the time.

The Crnojević and Vuković presses helped preserve the Montenegrins' national and religious spirit during Turkish invasions. The role they played in the history of Montenegrin culture can hardly be exaggerated.

The frescoes from the Church of St Basilius in Donji Stoliv, dating from the end of the 15th century, constitute an almost perfect symbiosis of the eastern and western styles of painting. Their inscriptions are in the Latin, Italian and Serbian languages, in Cyrillic and Latin script. The frescoes represent both Orthodox and Catholic saints.

214

The church in Morača monastery was refurbished at the close of the 16th century. Its iconostasis was made between 1596 and 1617. All the items in the church, including the beautiful ivory-decorated portal, were made during periods of Turkish rule. Their main purpose was to help Montenegrins endure the barbarity of their oppressors. In the flickering of candles and icon lamps, the figures and forms of Morača monastery create a magical atmosphere, as do the icons, frescoes and manuscripts in the churches of the Monastery of the Holy Trinity and Piva Monastery.

The walls of the Church of the Holy Trinity near Pljevlja are decorated with 16th-century fresco paintings of saints modelled on real people living in those days. Visitors observing the faces of these saints thus actually behold the faces of their own ancestors. Manuscript copying and book illumination were highly developed in this monastery.

Piva monastery is unique in that it was built with the permission of the Turkish rulers. Its construction lasted from 1573 to 1586, and its founder was the metropolitan of Herzegovina, Savatije, nephew of the Peć patriarch, Macarius, brother of Mehmed-Pasha Sokolović. There are representations of Savatije and Mehmed-Pasha above the southern portal of the church and in the frescoes. This is probably the only Orthodox church in the world adorned with a portrait of a Turk!

The Church of Our Lady of the Rocks on the man-made island off Perast is the largest treasury of Baroque art created in present-day Montenegro between the second half of the 17th century and the early 18th century. It is a true monument of Baroque painting. The entire loggia is decorated with 68 ceiling and wall canvases. They were made over a period of ten years by a Montenegrin, Tripo Kokolja, who adhered to the domestic tradition of painting but also drew on Venetian influences.

The Church of the Assumption, located within the grounds of Gradište monastery, is yet another monument of fresco art. The church is famous for its painting of a saint with a donkey's head, called "St Donkey". This artistic rarity presumably reflects the social changes at the time.

215

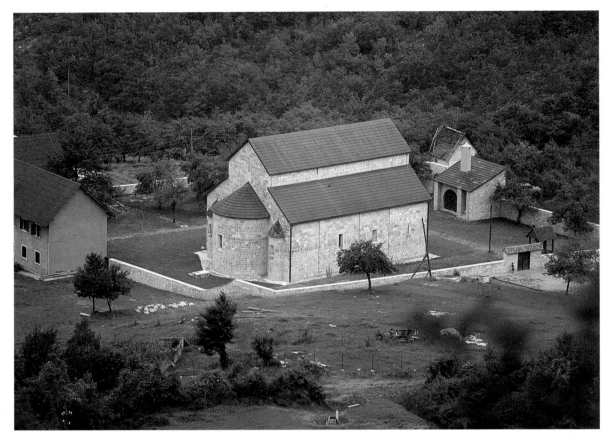

216.
The Piva
Monastery

217.
"Oktoih
prvoglasnik"
(Octoechos for
the first voices)
printed in
Cetinje in
1494;
collections of
State Museum
in Cetinje

The Kotor school of painters and wood engravers produced the Dimitrijević-Rafajlović family from Risan, a line of eleven icon and fresco painters active for almost two hundred years - from the end of the 17th century to the second half of the 19th century.

The Founding Charter of Cetinje monastery, as a very important document for Montenegrin cultural heritage, was printed by Ivan Crnojević in Obod on 4 January 1485. The Cetinje Chronicle, a collection of various manuscripts and historical records relevant to the Crnojević family, was written in this monastery in the 16th century.

In 1701, Bishop Danilo, continuing the tradition of the Crnojević family, founded a new monastery on the site of the former Crnojević palace. The Turks destroyed it in one of their raids on Cetinje, but it was rebuilt later in the same century.

The Wallach Church, built in the mid-15th century by shepherds tending the flocks of their feudal lords, is enclosed by a fence made of the barrels of rifles captured by Montenegrins in battles against Turks in the 19th century. It is a symbol of war and peace.

Many works by known and unknown artists and writers have stood the test of time and are now kept in monasteries and churches throughout Montenegro. They have found their place in Montenegro's great cultural heritage.

218. The Piva Monastery (built between 1573-1586)

219

219.
The Gospa od Škrpjela
(The Lady of Škrpjel - rock)
and Sveti Djordje (St. George) churches.
Built on an artificial islet off Perast,
The Lady of Škrpjel'sholds the largest
collection of baroque art in Montenegro
220.
Luxuriant ornaments in
The Lady of Škrpjel's
Church are the work of the
baroque painter Tripo Kokolja

221.
The Bay of Kotor with The Lady of
Škrpjel's and St. George's isles

220

221

222

222-224.
The Ostrog Monastery, near the village of Bogetići between Nikšić and Danilovgrad

ЦВѢТОНОСІЕ   ХВО

СТЫ ГЕѠРГІА СТЫ ДИМИТРІЕ СТЫ НЕСТОР

223

ІС ХС

224

225-227.
The Ostrog Monastery shelters the relics of St. Vasilije (Basil) - St. Vasilije Jovanović Ostroški
(b. Popovo Polje, 1610 - d. Ostrog, 1671) - the Metropolitan of Zahumlje. Curer and miracle-maker, the
founder of the Ostrog Monastery, St. Vasilije was a great man of exploit, a person with cardinal virtues, an
adamantine protector and defender of his people. After his demise his remains continued to act curatively.
St. Vasilije Ostroški is revered not only by the Orthodox but by other faiths as well, so Ostrog is visited
by pilgrims from all over the world.

227

228

Montenegrin national costumes:
228.
Vlaho Bukovac, "Guslar" (one-string fiddle player), 1917
229.
Jaroslav Cermak, "Princess Darinka, 1862
230.
Anton Karinger "The transfer of Prince Danilo's remains from Kotor to Cetinje", 1862
231.
Women's national costume belonging to one of the daughters of King Nikola
and
Men's national costume belonging to King Nikola

229

230

231

WRITERS AND ARTISTS

A small country, such as it is, Montenegro has nevertheless produced a large number of world-class artists and authors during its centuries-long struggle to survive.

Literature has always been highly valued in Montenegro. There is hardly another country with so many poets and prose writers as Montenegro relative to the total size of its population. There are about twenty state-owned and private publishing houses in Montenegro. Many of its writers have left an indelible imprint on its culture or have even become part of world literature.

Our selection must begin with The Epistles by Petar I, also known as St Petar of Cetinje, who lived in the 8th century. The spirit of independence that pervades this work encouraged Montenegrins to preserve the unity of their state and to uphold justice. The Epistles are like a biblical book of a more recent date through which Peter I defined the Montenegrin ethos.

Petar II Petrović Njegoš is a universal thinker and a superior lyrical and reflexive poet. His works, especially The Mountain Wreath, The Light of the Microcosm, and his will and correspondence are the highest achievements of Montenegrin literature and liberal thought. They constitute an aesthetic synthesis of reason and emotion, casting a distinctive light on man's place in nature and history. His most famous work, The Mountain Wreath, has been translated into nineteen languages and published in twenty-two countries in about fifty different editions.

Stjepan Mitrov Ljubiša and Marko Miljanov Popović were Montenegro's most famous self-taught authors.

Miljanov's Examples of Righteousness and Courage and his other works are in anecdotal form. His main precept is that moral and spiritual purposes are far more important than any material motives.

"Everything can be in short supply, even life itself, only righteousness must not be lacking," wrote Miljanov. To Miljanov, only the virtuous have the right to a future, and only a freer and more humane world merits existence.

The stories of Stjepan Mitrov Ljubiša and Marko Miljanov present morality in poetic form. Both writers used past events to show their fellow-countrymen what their future should be like. They sought ways to eliminate evil in man, which they saw as having a real existence in this world.

Nikola I Petrović's Poem to The Turk is unique in that it glorifies the bravery of the Turks, the age-old enemies of the Montenegrins. The Turk from the poem is an "eagle", a "knight" and a "terrible crown crusher", as opposed to Europe, which maligned him for centuries, while trembling before him all along. Although bitter foes, Montenegrins and Turks recognized each other's valour, respecting each other chivalrously.

Montenegro's most important modern authors of international fame are Mihailo Lalić, Borislav Pekić, Miodrag Bulatović and Danilo Kiš.

Mihailo Lalić (1914-1993) was one of the most eminent Yugoslav novelists. A World War II veteran, in his most important novels he paints a realistic picture of the war in the rough terrains of northern Montenegro. He wrote about the tragic times of occupation and the struggle between loyalty and betrayal. In his later works he treats Montenegro's more remote history. His works have been translated into twenty-one languages and have been published in twenty-five countries.

Borislav Pekić (1930-1992) was a novelist with a rare gift for sketching subtle psychological nuances and making sociological analyses pervaded with an ironic outlook on the world. An erudite and sophisticated thinker, "Pekić became familiar with entire historical epochs, revealing to us the hidden side of history." He spent many years living and working in London.

Miodrag Bulatović (1930-1991) was a writer famous for his unique imagination, peculiar style and brilliant rhetoric. His very first novels earned him international fame. Few Yugoslav authors have been so read, translated and represented in foreign encyclopedias as Bulatović.

Danilo Kiš (1935-1989), the "master of European literature", reached the height of his fame in the 1980s. His most prolific years were those spent in Paris. A winner of highest literary awards and often mentioned as a nominee for the Nobel prize for literature, Kiš was one of the world's most lucid and most eloquent post-World War II writers. Primarily a novelist, he was also a short-story writer, playwright, polemicist and translator. His works have been translated into seventeen languages. He was born in Serbia to a Hungarian father and a Montenegrin mother. He was educated in Cetinje, where he began his literary career. A great admirer of Njegoš, he regarded Montenegro as his homeland, while Montenegro loved him as one of its greatest sons.

Montenegro has also produced many internationally renowned artists in this century, notably Petar Lubarda, Milo Milunović, Miodrag Dado Đurić, Vojislav Stanić and Branko Filipović.

Petar Lubarda (1907-1974) was undoubtedly the greatest and most important of Montenegro's 20th-century artists. In his best works, made in the 1950s, he combined fresco painting with modern visual expressiveness, Montenegro's rugged landscapes with a modern visual logic.

Milo Milunović (1897-1967) is an artist of classical sensibility. His canvasses are a testimony to his patient quest for lost harmony in a dynamic century filled with tragedy and hope.

Miodrag Dado Đurić (1933) is an original interpreter of the world's apocalyptic destiny, a poet of destruction whose work is filled with delicate expressions of painful lyricism.

Vojislav Vojo Stanić (1924), a loner in self-imposed exile, is a painter of recognizable coastal ambiences, a lucid creator of an authentic visual expression, infinitely witty, but, above all, a great explorer of the unpredictable visual language. In contrast to Đurić, Branko Filipović-Filo (1924) is a poet of creation. A disciple of Lubarda's, he is a painter of positive energy and passionate life growth. His intense expressionist paintings are not only a testimony to his passionate sensibility but also to Montenegro's unique geography.

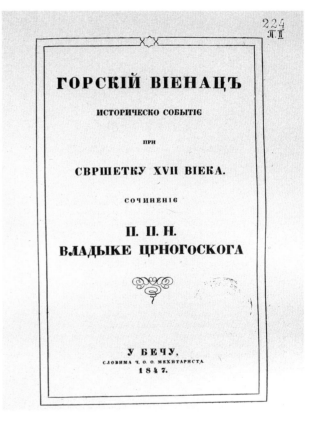

232.
"Gorski vijenac"
(The Mountain
Wreath),
a fascimile
edition of the
1847 original
printed in
Vienna;
collections of
Njegoš's
Museum

Artists, scholars and scientists from other Slav countries who lived and worked in Montenegro are also part of its cultural heritage. The same goes for numerous travel writers, painters, statesmen and explorers from non-Slav countries who visited Montenegro and made valuable records of its past.

These luminaries include Serbian cultural reformer Vuk Stefanović Karadžić, French author Prosper Mérimée, Russian poet Aleksandr Pushkin, English archaeologist Arthur Evans, English poet Alfred, Lord Tennyson, British politician William Gladstone, Italian botanist Antonio Baldacci, legal scholar Valtasar Bogišić, Chech painter Jaroslav Čermak, Russian scientist Pavle Rovinsky, Serbian authors Sima Milutinović Sarajlija, Djura Jakšić, Laza Kostić, Simo Matavulj and Ljubomir Nenadović, Chech botanist Joseph Rohlena, Chech composer Ludevit Kuba and Serbian historians Dimitrije Milaković and Dušan Vuksan.

MUSEUMS AND GALLERIES

Montenegro has a large number of national and local cultural institutions whose task is to preserve Montenegro's cultural heritage and promote culture and the arts.

Montenegro in its entirety is one big museum. Most of its cultural treasure is concentrated in Cetinje, its former capital. Some 400 cultural monuments in Montenegro are protected by law, and its museums and libraries are all open to visitors.

There are very good conditions for cultural activity, given Montenegro's ramified network of cultural institutions, theatres, publishing houses, cultural centres, galleries, artists' associations, cultural magazines, cinemas, radio and TV stations and educational centres.

Each municipality in Montenegro organizes an annual event dedicated to cultural activity attracting the largest number of enthusiasts in that community.

Particularly important are the events that bring together leading Yugoslav and foreign artists and authors. Most of these events take place in coastal towns in the summer, and the audiences always include large numbers of tourists. On these occasions culture becomes part of people's everyday life. Budva's drama festival called the Theatre City lasts fifty days and features renowned international theatrical and opera companies. Shakespeare's and Beckett's plays are performed in Budva's old town, and the festival's prizes are craved even by recognized artists and performers. A festival of poetry called Poets' Square turns every street in Budva into a scene of close encounters between poets and their audiences.

The International Summer Book Fair in Herceg Novi has in a very few years grown into a first-class cultural event. During its fifty-five days, the Bar Chronicle festival presents various artistic achievements from Yugoslavia. Many other cultural events are held in the summer, turning the whole of Montenegro into a great stage on which the line between performers and audiences becomes blurred.

If you look for an artistic act as a collective experience, you can find it in Montenegro. A harmonious combination of heritage and modern cultural activity makes Montenegro a rich source for all those listening to the whisper of the Muses.

233.
Fragments of a plaque (5-7th c.) found in Virpazar;
collections of State Museum in Cetinje

233

*The existing natural resources,
human potential, and the
created technical infrastructure
represent the basis
for economic
development and protecting
the environment in
Montenegro.*

*234.
Bridge over the Djurdjevića Tara*

THE ECONOMY AND DEVELOPMENT OPPORTUNITIES

As a relatively small princedom and kingdom, Montenegro made its first steps in organised economic development and industrialisation at the end of the nineteenth and beginning of the twentieth centuries. The causes of this tardiness mostly lie in the national efforts to ensure independence and the historical survival of the state. Alongside this there was little investment in the economy, the building of infrastructure, research of the raw materials available and training of people.

However this has had a very pronounced positive effect. Montenegro has survived as a unique ecological oasis. Thus it has gained one of the most significant stimuli for modern economic growth, whose success long term will only be measured by the ecological effects on current and future generations.

*235.
"Perper"
the first
coin in
Montenegro
(1902)*

ECONOMIC DEVELOPMENT

The international recognition of Montenegro as an independent country in 1878 at the Berlin Congress and the gaining of an exit to the sea were the two main preconditions for the building of the economy to start.

Montenegro very quickly adopted a constitution and formed a government which sought to create the economic conditions for growth.

Roads were built, the first factories, banks, and the Montenegrin currency ("Perper") introduced... International agreements were made with respect to trade and shipping, ports were opened for free transport and benefits were given to certain authorised nations in trade.

This short period of industrial evolution was interrupted by new wars. Between the two world wars as part of the Kingdom of Yugoslavia, Montenegro was predominantly agricultural, whilst industry was limited to a couple of factories for the processing of fertilizer, tobacco, and the production of beer and salt.

Only after the Second World War did real progress take place in the economy. Once again destroyed and abandoned, Montenegro invested effort in economic development, thus building the foundations for a modern and prosperous economy.

NATURAL AND CREATED RESOURCES

The existing natural resources, human potential, and the created technical infrastructure represent the basis for economic development and protecting the environment in Montenegro.

The geological structure of Montenegro ensures that in a very small land area is found an exceptionally rich source of raw materials. Rich and long profitable seams of red bauxite, led and zinc are being exploited. The main non-metal raw materials also exist: marl, decorative stone,

236.
*The Ulcinj
Saltworks*

clay for bricks, barite, bentonite, dolomite, quartz sand... The salinity of the sea and the climate are very favourable for traditional sea salt production, using sun energy. The main sources of coal have also been discovered and represent a significant energy potential. River flow offers twice the potential for generating electrical energy than is at present being exploited.

Agricultural land covers over a third of the total territory of Montenegro. Montenegro has the real potential to increase the existing potential (0.32 hectares per head) such that pastoral land would be converted to meadow, and meadow into arable fields or fruit orchards.

Forests cover as much as 40 percent of Montenegrin territory. Per head that is almost one hectare of forest. Over half the forests are protected, whilst the rest is used for economic activities, but under strict and special regulations which ensure they are renewable.

Alongside the forest potential there are over 400 various types of plant (medicinal, aromatic, edible, industrial...) which have wide applications. They grow at various heights above sea level and therefore have different periods of growth, which enables them to be utilised throughout the year.

As a result of the special climate, altitude, and protected zones, Montenegrin agriculture is involved in the production of natural organic foods and early vegetables. Regionally the main orientation is the production of southern fruits, and early vegetables along the coastal strip, continental fruit and vegetables in the lower areas of the central and northern regions, and dairy and meat products in the mountain areas.

Tourism has a high priority in Montenegro. Almost ideal conditions exist for both winter and summer tourism, including tourism on the coast and inland. Almost 140,000 beds are

available, primarily in the "B" category. On average annually about 10 million night stays are achieved, with a net income in convertible currency of 140 million US$. The opportunities for tourism development have not yet been sufficiently researched and evaluated, especially with regard to attractive coastal locations, mountains, winter, village and hunting tourism.

The coastal network of tourist centres includes Budva (a first class tourist centre), Herceg Novi, Kotor, Ulcinj and other smaller tourist places. The main areas of tourism in north Montenegro are the winter sports centres of Žabljak and Kolašin.

Merchant shipping has a very long tradition. As early as the 18th century over 400 ships from the Boka Kotor Bay sailed the world's oceans, and there were over 300 coastal lighters in use. Two significant shipping companies exist in Montenegro. Their fleets together represent over one million registered tonnes of shipping. The Montenegrin potential in this area takes in the port of Bar, the shipyards at Bijela and Tivat, various marinas, shipping agents, customs free zones, as well as shipping on Lake Skadar.

The transport system in Montenegro includes air, sea, road and rail networks.

Two "A" class airports are in operation. Flights enable communication with the whole of the world. Shipping is mainly concentrated in the port of Bar with a capacity of 4.5 million tonnes annual turnover of goods. Road and rail communications consist of a network of local and regional routes, as well as international corridors. Existing rail track is 249 kilometres long and is mainly electrified. The road network encompasses 5,174 kilometres, of which 3,085 km is modern asphalted surface.

The telecommunications network is based on modern and highly automated equipment. The electrical energy system is a technical and technological part of the Yugoslav and European system. Practically every location has electricity. Only a few distant mountain villages have still not been connected to the distribution system.

A high priority in the social and economic development of Montenegro has been given to housing, as a basic element of the standard of living of the population. So far an average of 18m2 of relatively comfortable living space per head has been achieved.

The social infrastructure for education and health must meet various performance targets. Basic education encompasses 98% of the generation (7 to 14 years), and secondary (high) school 60% of the generation (15 to 18 years). The teaching programmes are very ambitious. In primary school two foreign languages are part of the basic curriculum. A university education is offered by the University of Montenegro. Scientific research is carried out in various research institutions which are coordinated by the University and the Montenegrin Academy of Sciences and Arts.

The Health Service consists of a network of health centres which offer basic medical protection to the local population: special advice and health centres, specialized hospitals and clinics, general hospitals and clinical centres. It is able to offer complete health protection to both the general population and also to tourists staying in Montenegro. Each citizen enjoys a guaranteed level of free basic health protection.

Information is spread through daily newspapers, and hundreds of weeklies and magazines which are published in Montenegro. Radio and TV programmes cover directly or by relay 95% of the territory.

At the moment 12,552 companies are in operation in Montenegro in all areas of activity. Of these 11,320 are private and 717 are state-controlled with a majority state holding, these latter being in areas which touch on the basic foundation of the economy and strategic industry.

A NEW CONCEPT OF ECONOMIC DEVELOPMENT

A new concept of economic development implies balanced and sustainable growth with ecological criteria as decisive factors in the choice of projects. Montenegro represents an open economic region in which the market economy and the freedom of companies lend support to its ecological sovereignty.

The development strategy is based on existing potential and is oriented towards several vital economic areas. The priorities are in the development of tourism, agriculture and the production of "clean" energy and the maritime economy.

One of the most significant all-encompassing projects is "Montenegro - free economic zone". This foresees that Montenegro will become a new centre for international business operations, and will offer business, tourist and other services to foreign companies at the highest standards. "Montenegro - free economic zone" is a system of specific business regimes which will ensure an attractive ambiance to potential investors, offering significant tax benefits, no customs duties, easy repatriation of profits and other advantages. Special emphasis is being put on the international "off shore centre", for the formation of companies with specific purposes, and the creation of financial conditions such that Montenegro will be selected by many business people both as a place to do business in and as a pleasant place to stay.

One of the foundation stones of this new economic development concept is the intensifying of institutional relations with the European Union and regional organisations for cooperation in work-force training, inter-regional economic development and the attraction of investment.

The freedom and development of Montenegro, a state which has existed for centuries in the Balkans and Europe, is safeguarded in the modern conditions of civilisation both by the strength of its companies and by its citizens, doing business together with all those who wish to earn, respecting and advancing the environment, and by openness to cooperation with the whole world.

Especially with those who in a similar way love and look after their own homeland, in order to pass it on even more beautiful and richer to future generations.

237.
Sveti Stefan
238.
Ada Bojana (island) near Ulcinj
239.
Sutomore, a tourist resort near Bar

*The oldest living olive tree
in Europe grows in Mirovica,
near Bar, southern Montenegro.
Planted 2,500 years ago,
it still produces fruit.
This exquisite symbol
of life's permanence has witnessed
the disappearance of a multitude
of monuments belonging
to Montenegro's diverse
yet intertwining
cultures.*

100

IMPORTANT DATES IN MONTENEGRIN HISTORY

1. 6th c.: After the fall of Sirmium (582) the Slavs and the Avars started settling on the southern parts of the Balkans, taking the territory of the present-day Montenegro.

2. 6-8th c.: During the Slavic colonization nine "župa"s (administrative units, districts) populated mainly with Slavic tribes were founded in the state of Doclea.

3. 6-7th c.: Prevalitana (Roman name for the district of Prevalis): a Slavic region of Doclea corresponding to the heart of the Roman empire.

4. 1042: The battle of Bar in which the prince of Zeta Vojislav defeated the Byzantine army. A rapid rise of Doclea began then.

5. 1080: The name Zenta (Kekavmen, Gentta) was used for the first time, while the Bar Chronicle uses the name Zeta (chapter XXX).

6. 1081: Zetan ruler Mihailo was the first to be given the title of king.

7. 1180: The Bar Chronicle (Chronicle of the Doclean Priest): a historic document containing the accounts of early feudal states in the Balkans.

8. 1185: Grand "župan" (chieftain, district prefect) Stefan Nemanja annexed Zeta to Raška.

9. 1195: Nemanja's son Vukan was appointed to govern Zeta with the title of king. Thus Zeta remained within the Nemanjićs' state until the rise of local lords when it became part of the "Despotovina"- Serbian despotic state - from which it was detached at the time of the Crnojevićs in early 15th century.

10. 1219: Zeta Episcopate (bishopric) founded within the Serbian Orthodox Church, with the seat at Prevlaka near Tivat.

11. 1262: "Ilovačka krmčija" a manuscript with civil-church laws of the Zetan bishop Neofil.

12. 1282-1321: The name of "Crna Gora" (Montenegro) was for the first time used in a charter of King Milutin. The second mention of Montenegro was made in 1435 in a compact between Djurdje Branković and the Venet ians. As a geographic term, the name "Crna Gora" was permanently established in 14th century.

13. 1360-1421: Zetan dynasty of the Balšićs (Balša I, Balša II, Balša III) ruled Zeta as district governors.

14. 1441-1442: "Gorički zbornik" (Gorica Collection) - the correspondence between Jelena Balšić and monk Nikon of Jerusalem - came to be; the original is kept in the archives of the Serbian Academy of Sciences and Arts "SANU").

15. 1475: The town of Obod ("Riječki grad") was founded. Later, the ruler of Zeta Ivan Crnojević had his seat there, it was the seat of the Zeta Metropolitan, and by one claim the first Cyrillic printing shop opera ted there as well.

16. 4/1/1485: Ivan Crnojević chartered the building of the Cetinje Monastery ("as the seat of Cetinje Metropolitan, that is of Zeta Metropolitan"). Cetinje afterwards became the seat of Zetan rulers and its Metrop olitan.

17. 1/7/1490: Djuradj Crnojević, son of Ivan, came to rule Zeta. A man with the renaissance education, knew Latin and Greek as well as mathematics and astronomy, he reigned until 1496.

18. 1494: Printing of "Oktoih" - the first Cyrillic book among the southern Slavs - was completed in Cetinje. It is a service book produced with a marvelous technique by the masterly hand of the renow ned printer monk Makarije.

19. 1498: In the administrative-territorial division of the Ottoman Empire Montenegro was attached to the Skadar sanjak as a separate "kadiluk" (area under the jurisdiction of one magistrate - kadi).

20. 1513: Skender-bey - the Islamized son of Ivan Crnojević - was appointed the sanjak-bey (governor) of Montenegro which thus became a separate sanjakate.

21. 1597: The uprising of Nikšić "vojvoda" (duke) Grdan against the Turks. It was one of crucial moments in the creation of anti-Osmanli feeling in the western Christian states.

22. 1611: Bosnian pasha with 40,000 soldiers undertook an offensive against the rebelling highland tribes among which the Bjelopavlićs were to suffer most heavily.

23. 1638: Montenegrin "vladika " (arch) bishop - Mrdarije accepted to negotiate the union with the Roman curia.

24. 1662: In Kolašin, the sanjak-bey of Herzegovina had 57 princes and other chieftains from Nikšić, Piva and Drobnjak executed.

25. 20/3/1688: (The tribe of) Kuči defeated Suleiman-pasha's army.

26. Dec. 1689: The Montenegrins and the Venetians captured the stronghold of Mustapha Mehmed-bey at Rijeka Crnojevića, thus breaking one of important bases of the Osmanli rule in Montenegro.

27. 1697: At a pan-Montenegrin assembly Danilo Šćepčević was elected the secular lord, and at the Pecs Synode in 1700 he was ordained "vladika". He is the founder of the dynasty that was to rule Montenegro until the loss of its independent statehood.

28. 1707: "Montenegrin Vespers" of Christmas Eve (mass slaughter of those who had converted to Islam). Some noted historians call the event a popular revolution: it had begun against converted compatriots coming to mean the unsparing war against the Osmanli empire.

29. June 1711: Political links between Montenegro and Russia were established with the arrival of the Russian tzar's envoy.

30. Jul-Aug. 1712: The battle of Carev Laz against the troops of Bosnian vizier

Ahmet-pasha. In the consciousness of the nation the event ranks as one of the greatest victories in the history of Montenegrin warfare.

31. 1713: Montenegrin assembly elected the All-state Court of twelve members chaired by Vukadin Vukotić.The Court was an important institute of promoting the idea and creating the tradition of statehood in the more recent history of Montenegro.

32. 1714: Ćuprilić's attack on Montenegro was both in retaliation for the failure of Ahmet-pasha's offensive (1712) and the sultan's wish to suppress at any price the heart of resistance in this part of the Balkans.

33. 1715: "Vladika "Prince-Bishop - Danilo I visited Petersburg and was received by Russian Tzar Peter the Great. That was a hint of the future orientation in the foreign policy of Montenegro in which Russian influence was to play a decisive role all until the loss of Montenegro's independence.

34. 21/6/1718: The Treaty of Požarevac: Venice got Grbalj, Majine, Pobori, Brajići, Krivošije, Ubli and Ledenice. The new border was called "The Mochenigo Line" after the Venetian general proveditor in Zadar.

35. 1754: "The History on Montenegro" published in Moscow. Its author, Bishop Vasilije, thus became the progenitor of Montenegrin historiography.

36. 10-21/3/1766: Vasilije Petrović had died in Petersburg and was buried in the Blagovješćenska (Annunciation) Cathedral.

37. 25/9/1767: By the gates of Budva the decree of Šćepan Mali (The Small) was read announcing "a new age in Montenegro". Šćepan was a pretender who claimed to be the Russian emperor Peter III.

38. 1782: Petar I Petrović Njegoš (Nyegosh) became the secular lord (reigned until 1830) and in 1784, in Sremski Karlovci, was ordained archbishop.

39. 1785: The campaign of the Skadar vizier on Montenegro: Cetinje was burnt, the monastery razed and its treasury plundered.

40. 30/6-11/7/1796: The battle of Martinići: the Montenegrins and the Highlanders defeated the Turkish army, wounding its chief commander.

41. 6-17/8/1796: "Stega", the first legal act, was enacted; it bound the Montenegrins and the Highlanders by oath to joint political and military actions.

42. 3/10/1796: The battle of Krusi: a turning point in the historical development of Montenegro. The Montenegrins won a glorious victory: the vizier of Skadar Mahmut-pasha Bushatlia was killed, and after that Montenegr o entered the world as a "de facto" independent state.

43. 1798: "Praviteljstvo "(judges) of the Court of Montenegro and the Highlands was established (i.e.appointed) headed by Prince-Bishop Petar I. It was the first body of the central rule/government in the proce ss of constituting a modern Montenegrin state.

44. 1798: The chieftains assembly at the village of Stanjevići passed the first part - seventeen articles - of the General Statute of Montenegro and the Highlands.

45. 1803: The second part - 33 articles - of the Statute of Montenegro and the Highlands was passed.

46. 1806: Montenegro came into conflict with France upon the appeal made by the population of Boka Kotorska at the Assembly of Risan.

47. 1806: The Montenegrins and the people from Boka, together with Russian soldiers of Senyavin's fleet, fought the French, taking Cavtat and beginning the siege of Dubrovnik.

48. Sep.1806: The battle of Herceg Novi: marshal Marmont's troops suffered heavy losses and the Montenegrin-Boka's and Russian armies managed to defend the town.

49. 1809: In response to Karageorge's appeal, Petar I sent his troops to meet the rebels.

50. 29/10/1813: The Assembly of Dobrota (near Kotor) proclaimed the union of Montenegro and Boka Kotorska and elected a provisional government headed by Petar I.

51. 1820: The battle on the River Morača: the Montenegrins defeated the Turkish army and formally joined the regions of Rovca and Morača to their state.

52. 1830: Petar II Petrović Njegoš came to rule, which lasted until 1850.

53. 1831: "Praviteljstvujušći" (just, honourable) Senate of Montenegro and the Highlands was established with Ivan Vukotić as Chairman and Matija Vučićević as Vice-chairman. Also "Gvardija" (court of first instance) and "Perjanik's (the guard) were instituted.

54. 1834: A printing house was established in Cetinje; it produced Vuk Karadžić's (Dictionary) and Prince-Bishop's "Pustinjak cetinjski" (The Hermit of Cetinje).

55. 1834: The first elementary school started in Cetinje.

56. 1835: The first yearly magazine "Grlica" (Dove) was printed. Five volumes were published altogether.

57. 1841: A treaty on demarcation was signed between Montenegro and Austria. The border established then was not changed until the loss of Montenegrin sovereignty.

58. 1842: Petar II and Ali-pasha signed a treaty by which Montenegro was for the first time deisgnated as "the independent district".

59. 1847: "Gorski vijenac " (The Mountain Wreath), the most famous work of the greatest Montenegrin poet, philosopher, and Prince-Bishop Petar II Petrović Njegoš, was published for the first time in Vienna.

60. 1851: Danilo II Petrović came to power; ruled until 1860.

61. 1852: Montenegro proclaimed Princedom. Russian government accepted the proposal of the Montenegrin Senate for the change of the form of government, and since then a secular supreme rule was formally consti tuted in Montenegro.

62. 1855: "Danilov zakonik" (Danilo's Code) was passed; it meant the final stage in the process of establishing the state order in Montenegro.

63. 1-13/5/1858: The battle of Grahovo, recorded in popular memory as an event of fateful importance for the definitive recognition of Montenegro's independence.

64. 8/11/1858: The Conference of Carigrad (Istanbul): the borders of Montenegro were established and recognized by the representatives of great powers. The following year the International Commission carried out the demarcation on site and fixed the state borders of Montenegro.

65. 1860: Prince Nikola Petrović came to power (1860-1918).

66. 1862: The war between Montenegro and Turkey: Montenegro suffered heavy losses (around 6,000 casualties) while considerable losses were inficeted upon the Ottoman army.

67. 1862: The Treaty of Rijeka Crnojevića was an act adverse by its content for Montenegro due to the provisions on the expulsion of Grand Duke Mirko and on the right of the Ottoman administration to erect fortifications along the Spuž-Nikšić road. Supported by Russia, Montenegro managed to nullify these provisions.

68. 23/9-5/10/1866: The agreement on alliance between Montenegro and Serbia: it was the first joint agreement that emphasized the principles of national-liberation programmes of both the countries.

69. 1874: "Knjaževska kancelarija" - Prince's Office - For Foreign Affairs was opened.

70. 28/5-9/6/1876: Secret Agreement On The Union of Montenegro and Serbia and Secret Military Convention between these two states were concluded. These documents provided the international and legal bases for politica l and military cooperation in the "Great War" (1876-1879).

71. 28/7/1876: The battle of Vučji Do took place at the beginning of the "Great War"; its outcome foretold the triumphant course of the war.

72. 14/8/1876: The battle of Fundina in which the units of the Montenegrin southern front, themselves having numerous casualties, inflicted a crushing defeat on the Turkish army, is the second greatest Montenegrin victory at the outbreak of the war.

73. 4/6/1877: The battle of Krstac: although suffering heavy casualties, the Montenegrins defeated the advance guard of "mušir " (marshal) Suleiman-pasha.

74. 17-25/6/1877: Nine bloody days: the most fierce battle fought on the Montenegrin-Turkish battlefield. Suleiman-pasha's army suffered very heavy losses due to which he was not able to undertake further o ffensive actions.

75. 24/6/1877: The battle on the Morača: the Montenegrins defeated a column of the Turkish army on its way to meet Suleiman-pasha's units. Miljan Vukov Vešovic's exceptional military talent was demonstrated in this battle.

76. 1877: Nikšić was liberated from Turkish rule, as well as Bar and Ulcinj (8/11/1877, 9/1/1878, and 18-19/1/ 1878, respectively).

77. 13/6/1878: By the decisions of the Congress of Berlin, Montenegro received international recognition. Its territory was doubled in size.

78. 1879: The Senate was dissolved and five ministries set up: of the army, of finances, of justice, of the internal and of foreign affairs.

79. 1879: Diplomatic relations were established with all major powers - Russia, France, Italy, Great Britain, Austria-Hungary, Turkey - except Germany.

80. 1880: The first secondary school in Montenegro - a "gimnazija" (grammar or comprehensive school) - was opened.

81. 1888: "Opšti imovinski zakonik" (General Property Code) was passed; it is a masterpiece of Valtazar Bogišić, one of the most learned European lawyers at the turn of the century. This law codifed the customary legal norms, accepting the principles of European civil canons but also expounding to the greatest possible extent the principles that Bogišić himself had created and the Montenegrin legal practice accepted.

82. 1905: The Constitutional Assembly was convened and the first Constitution adopted; it was composed after the Serbian Constitution of 1903, but in certain solutions (eg. the property census) it went a step forward.

83. 1908: The agreement on alliance between Montenegro and Serbia was signed on the occasion of the annexation crisis.

84. 28/8/1910: Montenegro was proclaimed Kingdom.

85. 1912: The agreement on alliance with Serbia and Bulgaria was made.

86. 1912-1913: The First and the Second Balkan Wars ended with the treaties of London and Bucharest.

87. 1913: The agreement on demarcation between Montenegro and Serbia reached.

88. 1914: Montenegro entered the war immediately following the Austro-Hungarian declaration of war on Serbia, accepting the joint war plan and carrying out the wartime mobilization. The most elite units of its army were sent to Sandžak and Bosnia as a strategic reserve to the Serbian army.

89. 1916: The battle of Mojkovac: final operations of the Sandžak units, by which the role of their strategic support to Serbian army was successfully completed.

90. 1916-1918: The "komiti" (guerilla) movement started in Montenegro; in many respects it appeared to be a true free army in the occupied Europe.

91. 13-26/11/1918: The Assembly of Podgorica was held; it decided that Montenegro make a union with Serbia and as such join the new Yugoslav state.

92. 1918-1929: Montenegro was one of the 32 administrative units of the Kingdom of Serbs, Croats and Slovenes.

93. 1929-1941: Montenegro was a constituent part of Zetska "banovina" (province) the territory of which was reduced by the Cvetković-Maček agreement.

94. 13/7/1941: The uprising of the Montenegrin people against the Italian occupiers. The dominant role in the event was played by the Communist Party of Yugoslavia, and by the massive participation and the liberation-determined energy, the uprising offers a unique example in Europe.

95. 1942: The liberation forces comprised 52 "partisan" batallions out of which three elite "proletarian" brigades were formed; two batallions (1st and 2nd) operated within the First Proletarian Brigade.

96. 1943 "CASNO" Montenegrin Antifascist Assembly of National Liberation met in Kolašin to give its support to the liberation struggle of other Yugoslav peoples, declare readiness to endure in the mutual struggle against the occupying forces, as well as in the creation of a common - federal - Yugoslav state.

97. 1945-1990: Montenegro was one of the six federal units - republics - of the Socialist Federal Republic of Yugoslavia.

98. 20/9/1991: The Assembly (Parliament) of the Republic of Montenegro met at Žabljak to adopt a declaration on proclaiming Montenegro the Ecological State.

240. Herceg Novi today

99. 1/3/1992: A popular referendum took place: the people decided that Montenegro, as a sovereign state, continue its existence within the joint state -Federal Republic of Yugoslavia.

100. 12/10/1992: The Parliament of Montenegro adopted the Constitution of the Republic of Montenegro, establishing it as a state of sovereign citizens, multy-party parliamentary democracy and market economy.

MONTENEGRO
ecological state

Published by
UNIREKS - PODGORICA
"13 jul", 27, 81000 Podgorica, phone/fax: 38181/45-095
For the publisher
JANKO BRAJKOVIĆ, Director

Project Editor
The STRUGAR STUDIO
Majke Jevrosime 14 a, 11000 Beograd, phone/fax: 38111/32-46-924
Director
VLATKA RUBINJONI STRUGAR

Translator
GAVIN BROWN
Captions and "100 Important Dates" translated by
DRAGAN VUGDELIĆ

Assistants
OLIVERA MILIĆ, Operative Editor
PAVLE PERENČEVIĆ, Assistant Translator
SANJA ĐURIŠIĆ, Proof Reader
BRATISLAV STOJADINOVIĆ, Assistant Photographer
MIŠO ĐUROVIĆ, Type Setting

Printed by
INCAFO, ARCHIVO FOTOGRAFICO, S.L. MADRID, 1996

CIRCULATION 20,000, in Serbian, English and German

C   UNIREKS, Podgorica 1996

ISBN 86-427-0543-4

CIP - Katalogizacija u publikacji
Centralne narodne biblioteke Republike
Crne Gore "Đurđe Crnojevic" - Cetinje

908 (497.16)

BULATOVIĆ, Momir
Montenegro - Ecological State / Momir Bulatović
; [contributors Milo Đukanovic ... [st al.]; translator
Gavin Brown, captions and "100 Important Dates" transleted
by Dragan Vugdelic] ; Photography Branislav Strugar. -
Podgorica: Unireks, 1996 (Madrid: INCAFO Archivo fotografico).
: Unireks, 1996 (Madrid: INCAFO Archivo fotografico)
-280 str. : ilustr. : 30 cm
Tiraž 5000.
ISBN 86-427-0540-X
1. Strugar, Branislav
P.k. : a) Crna Gora

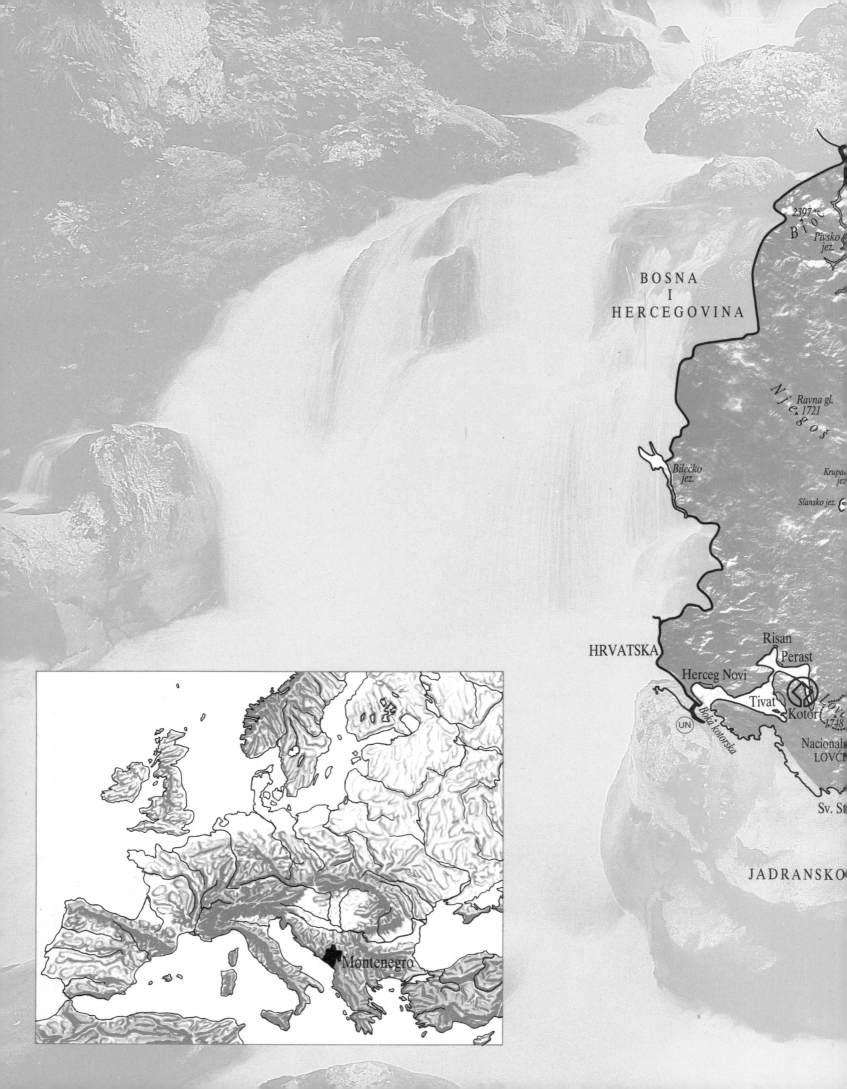

BOSNA
I
HERCEGOVINA

2397

B I O

Pivsko
jez.

Nj
e
g
o
š

Ravna gl.
1721

Bilećko
jez.

Krupa
jez

Slansko jez.

HRVATSKA

Risan
Perast

Herceg Novi

Tivat

Kotor

LOV
1748

UN

Boka kotorska

Nacional
LOVĆ

Sv. St

JADRANSKO

Montenegro